DISTANCE EDUCATION

Distance Education
Origin, Growth and Development

P. Satyanarayana
C. Sesharatnam
Emmanuel DK Meduri

SHIPRA

Rs.1250

ISBN: 978-81-7541-810-3

First Published in India in 2015

Distance Education: Origin, Growth and Development

Published by:

SHIPRA PUBLICATIONS

LG 18-19, Pankaj Central Market,
I.P. Ext., Patparganj, Delhi 110092, India
Ph.: +91 11 22235152; 9650028065
Email: info@shiprapublication.com
www.shiprapublication.com

Dedicated to the
Memory of
Prof. G. Ram Reddy
Architect of India's Open University System

Contents

Introduction

Many professionals, practitioners and students today wish to know something of distance education. Distance education is a great educational innovation of recent period. It has been rapidly expanding in the developed and developing countries. It has created enormous opportunities for the expansion of educational opportunities, especially at the higher education levels.

Distance education is a method of imparting knowledge, skills and attitudes which is rationalised by the application of division of labour and organization principles as well as by the extensive use of technical media, especially for the purpose of producing and reproducing high quality teaching material which makes it possible to instruct greater number of students at the same time wherever they live.

Distance education now holds the key to an educational revolution that will see access expanded, quality enhanced and cost reduced. By using technology of distance education wider access, high quality and lower cost occur all at the same time. This is a revolution, which never happened before.

Distance education has been playing several key roles in a modern education system such as balancing inequalities between age groups, offering second chance upgrading, speedy and efficient training of key target groups, expanding the capacity for education in new areas, offering the combination of education with work, and developing multiple competencies.

A student of distance education needs to have a reasonable degree of familiarity with the theory, the general principles of material production, delivery, management and support systems. This book aims to help the reader gain such familiarity.

This work begins with origin and development of distance education: When it began? Where it began? and how it began? This provides the historical background to the growth of distance education. Like other educational fields, distance education is also based on certain theories. The important theories are described in this work. Distance education providers are not of one type.

Different types of institutions are evolved over the time. These are dealt in the section on classification of distance education institutions. One of the most striking international developments in higher education in the recent past has been the establishment of a significant number of distance teaching universities, which are popularly called Open Universities. Organisation, policies and practices of these universities are also described here.

The other components of distance education – distance courses, distance students, multi media instructional system, student support system, staff development, etc., are also dealt with in this book.

Various information and communication technologies used for distance teaching and learning, mainly audio, video and computer technologies, are briefly described here.

The last part deals with quality assurance and leadership in distance education. At the end, names of organizations, associations and journals in distance education are given.

We have not attempted to provide a comprehensive work on distance education theory and practice. This book is meant as an introduction to the study of distance education. For further understanding of the emerging and rapidly spreading distance education, we advise readers to study works authored by leading theoreticians and practitioners of distance education.

1

Distance Education
Origin and Development

Distance education has been growing fast, in a marvelously diverse fashion, around the world. This is evidenced by:

- A large number of individual institutions are coming up to provide distance education.
- Many State funded distance education institutions are being setup throughout the world.
- Several national parliaments and provincial legislatures are favouring the creation of distance education institutions.
- Distance education has been recognized as an integral and valued component of many educational systems.
- The efficiency, effectiveness, validity, reliability and utility of distance education are on increase.

Concept of Distance Education

The term 'distance education' in English is of quite recent origin. When the International Extension College came into being in England at the beginning of 1971, this term did not exist. People talked about 'correspondence education' to describe the method of teaching through printed materials, sent by post to students who studied them and sent back exercises or assignments to their tutors who in turn marked and returned them by post. In the Christian tradition, one of the earliest and most significant efforts at religious education was the letters of St. Paul. The Islamic tradition records that the Prophet himself conveyed much of his teaching to followers who lived away from him by letters. Correspondence education in the modern form, however, began in the middle of the nineteenth century.

References to what probably correspondence education was occurred as early as 1720s and to what was indisputably correspondence education in the 1830s. Correspondence education is teaching in writing, by means of so called self-instructional texts, combined with communication in writing, i.e., correspondence between students and tutors. There were thus two constituent elements of correspondence education. As media other than the written word became common and grew in importance, the term correspondence education was felt by many to be narrow. Distance education is the designation that has gradually been adopted in the United Kingdom (though resisted by the Association of British Correspondence Colleges), in North America, Australia, New Zealand, and other parts of the English-speaking world, as well as internationally. Usage in this context can be studied in the periodicals concerned with this type of education. 'Distance' occurs in the very first issue of the British Open University journal 'Teaching at a Distance' and in the names of the Australian journal 'Distance Education', the Canadian journal 'Journal of Distance Education', and the USA journal 'American Journal of Distance Education'. A degree of formal recognition of the term distance education occurred in 1982 when the International Council for Correspondence Education (ICCE) changed its name to the International Council for Distance Education (ICDE). Later, the name was changed to International Council for Open and Distance Education.

Distance Education is a generic term and includes a wide range of teaching-learning strategies. It is known by a variety of names such as 'home study' at further educational level and 'independent study' at higher education level in the United States; as 'external studies' in Australia; 'outreach', 'extra mural system', and 'off-campus programme' in some countries. In French it is referred to as 'teleenseignement', 'Fernstudium' in German; 'education a distancia' in Spanish and 'teleducacao' in Portuguese.

Comparison with Face-to-Face (Conventional) Education

Ripley Sims (1977), who contributed a valuable study of distance education processes, had drawn a border line between distance education (which he calls correspondence education) and conventional education. The basic difference he felt, is in means of communication.

> "In the contiguous learning environments, communication is personal and face-to-face; in the non-contiguous environments communication may be personal and face-to-face for limited periods of time, but it is largely written, mechanical, electronic or

> some other means of communicating at a distance...... Learning is fundamentally an individual process and each person enters the process with techniques and levels of achievement uniquely his own. The method of correspondence study provides simultaneously an educational device for individualization in three distinct senses – student ability, variety of course offerings and flexibility for time and place of study.

Peters (1988), who is seriously concerned with the differences between distance education and conventional education, viewed distance education as an industrialized form of teaching and learning.

Childs (1963) commented on conventional education in the following words:

> "Conventional teaching and learning, makes use of concepts of learning and teaching that have preserved the old mystiques that have maintained space-time barriers to learning."

Cropley and Kahl (1983), focused on the difference in psychological assumptions of the face-to-face and distance education systems. The differences viewed by them are given in their own words here:

Max Rowe has written cogently on the characteristics of distance (or indirect) education contrasted with those of conventional (or direct) teaching. Based on Rowe's papers, characteristics of the two approaches are given in the next page.

Kaye and Rumble (1978) also distinguished some of the main differences between conventional system (formal classroom based instruction) and distance learning system as shown on the next page.

Development of Distance Education

When organized distance education first occurred is not clear. The earliest mention, so far known of it, is found in 'The Boston Gazette' of 20 March 1728, in which 'Caleb Phillips, teacher of the new method of Short Hand' advertised that any 'person in the country desirous to learn this art, may be having the several lesson sent weekly to them, be as perfectly instructed as those that live in Boston'. Some doubt whether this information really concerned distance education. However, the date is worth noting as it refers to new type of education activity. About a hundred years later, we find more conclusive evidence of distance education in our sense. An advertisement in English in "Lunds Weckoblad", No. 30, 1833, a weekly published in the old Swedish University city of Lund, offered to "Ladies

Face-to-face Education and Distance Education

Face-to-Face Education		Distance Education
Immediate personal contact between learner and teacher	1	Contact through communications media
Teacher can readily adapt to learners' immediate behaviour	2	Adaptation delayed
Learners environment is primarily designed to support learning activities	3	Learners environment is designed to serve other purposes (distracters)
Meta communication between teacher and learner is possible	4	Meta communication is difficult
Personal relationships can moderate learning	5	Personal relationship is of little importance
Direct Control of learner by teacher is possible	6	Teacher's influence is indirect
Learning materials can be of didactic standard	7	Learning materials must be of high didactic standard (well organised, clear, etc)
Learners experience limited degree of freedom	8	Learners experience of high degree of freedom
Wide opportunities exist for imitation/identification learning	9	Few opportunities exist for imitation/identification learning
Information is provided by a mixture of cues (Personal content-related, organization related)	10	Information is mainly provided by content and organization
Communication need not be planned to last detail	11	Communication is usually provided
A high degree of evaluation and feedback from the teacher is possible	12	A comparatively low degree of evaluation and feed-back from the teacher is possible
Internal motivation, self-direction, self-evaluation, planning, etc. can be low	13	Internal motivation, self-direction, self-evaluation, planning ability, etc. must be high
Willingness and ability of learner to work without direct supervision may be low	14	Willingness and ability of learner to work without direct supervision must be high

and Gentlemen" an opportunity to study composition through the medium of the Post.

Another early attempt to organize distance education was made in England by Isaac Pitman who reduced the main principles of his shorthand system to fit into postcards. He sent these to students who were invited to transcribe into shorthand short passages of the Bible and to be sent to him for correction. This teaching of shorthand combined with a study of the Scriptures began in the year 1840, when in the United Kingdom the uniform penny postage was introduced. In 1843 the Phonographic Correspondence Society was formed to take over these corrections of

Conventional Education and Distance Education

Conventional Education (Direct)		Distance education (Indirect)
Face-to-face, from teacher to student, with opportunities for direct interaction	1	Indirect communication by media with little or no direct interaction
Suitable for transmitting norms and attitudes	2	Suitable for transmitting knowledge and, to a limited extent, skills
Teacher is presenter of information which is often chosen by himself	3	Teacher is expert; tutor is the manager of instruction usually planned and produced by others
Compulsory attendance is the norm	4	Relies on high motivation and self discipline
Classroom is the locus of teaching activities	5	Learning occurs where ever the learner chooses to study
Definite schedule and rhythms of teaching	6	Self-paced at any time of day or week
A social process in association with others	7	Mostly a solitary process
Labour intensive	8	Capital Intensive
Decentralised costs rise with increasing number of learners	9	Centralised, costs fall with the increase of learners
Teacher-pupil ratio is generally low	10	Ratio is generally high
Depends on competence of the individual teacher with emphasis on the act of teaching	11	Draws on greatest experts working in a team but focuses on the individual student's learning needs and styles.

shorthand exercises. It was the beginning of what was later to become Sir Isaac Pitman Correspondence Colleges.

Organized distance education was introduced in Germany in 1856 by the Frenchman Charles Toussaint and the German Gustav Langenscheidt, who formed and organized a school in Berlin for language teaching, by correspondence.

In an advertisement published in 1898 it was claimed that the method of correspondence education was invented in Japan in 1882.

Among British pioneering organizations were:

- Skerry's college, Edinburgh, 1878.
- Foulks Lynch Correspondence Tuition Service, London, 1884.
- University Correspondence College, Cambridge, 1887.
- Diploma Correspondence College (Now called Wolsey Hall) Oxford, 1894.

The University of London under its first charter was limited to conduct examinations and to confer degrees. Teaching was the responsibility of its constituent colleges and students, desired to appear

Conventional and Distance-Learning Systems

Dimensions	*Conventional System*	*Distance-learning System*
1. Students	▪ relatively homogeneous (age and qualifications) ▪ same location (e.g. classrooms) ▪ largely 'dependent' learners ▪ controlled situation	▪ probably heterogeneous ▪ scattered, at-a-distance ▪ independent uncontrolled
2. Student Records	▪ do not need to be highly developed nor very detailed	▪ accurate ... student records essential (addresses, allocation to tutors, assessment grades, correspondence etc)
3. Student Support	▪ automatically built-in to face-to-face systems	▪ need for special provision of local back-up services to help students with learning problems and to minimise drop-out ▪ way of bridging the gap between student and central institution need to be designed ▪ distance implies control and response (time) problems to be met
4. Student Assessment and Accreditation	▪ problems of validity and reliability minimised ▪ relatively 'cheat-proof'	▪ assessment at-a-distance increase problems of validity ▪ use of large numbers of correspondence tutors decreases reliability (need for monitoring procedures) ▪ cheating/impersonation a potential problem: credibility
5. Media/ Methods	▪ essentially face-to-face teaching ▪ labour intensive ▪ teaching skills needed fairly well defined	▪ essentially 'mediated' teaching ▪ capital intensive ▪ skills needed generally not readily available
6. Courses	▪ relatively simple, few, and well-defined creation, production and distribution processes ▪ low start-up but high student-variable costs: tendency for many options courses with a few students on each	▪ more complex, course creation-production-distribution processes, with specialized staff functions arising from divisions of labour ▪ high start-up costs but low student-variable costs: tendency for few options with many students per course, to achieve economies of scale (if latter an objective)
7. Organization Administration	▪ little administrative support: vast majority of staff in schools and colleges are the teachers	▪ strong administrative framework needed to link together student support and record functions, course creation functions, course production and distribution functions (industrial and quasi-industrial processes)

Dimensions	*Conventional System*	*Distance-learning System*
	▪ main administrative problems are concerned with time-tabling of teaching periods and with management of teaching staff (personnel functions)	▪ some specialist functions may need to be carried out outside the DLS (e.g. printing, broadcasting)
8. Control and Regulation	▪ conventional problems of planning, scheduling, evaluation, leadership, decision-making	▪ these problems are magnified and in certain cases are qualitatively different (e.g. the capital intensive and multimedia nature of institution imposes longer planning horizons on many more fronts; integration of multimedia creation production-distribution and teaching systems imposes production control)
9. Cost Structure	▪ basically labour-intensive, and directly and primarily related to numbers of students; unit costs per student/year do not vary significantly with numbers per course	▪ basically capital-intensive, and related more to course creation and production costs than to student costs; unit costs per student/year drop significantly with increased numbers per course

for an examinations had to follow a course of study at one of these. In 1858, this restriction was removed and any person could be admitted for a degree. This led the way for matriculation of external students. The University had no responsibility for teaching them and private correspondence colleges provided opportunities and to prepare those external students, who wanted this form of help for the University of London examinations. In 1898 the University was reconstituted and began to teach internal students through its recognized schools and colleges while retaining the continuing responsibility for the examination of external students, the majority of whom were self-taught or prepared by one of commercial correspondence colleges.

The idea that, universities should involve in extension activity, first emerged in the early 1870s at the University of Cambridge but subsequently lost importance. In 1884 the leaders of the British University Extension movement pressed for a 'part-time, non-residential teaching university operating a system of academic credits'. Somehow the movement did not succeed and the idea was considered to be ahead of its time. Richard Moulton, a leader of the movement later went to USA and helped William Rainey Harper in setting up the Extension Department at the newly established University of Chicago.

Three nineteenth century British Universities had a particularly strong concern with 'openness'. They together enabled many thousands of people to study and obtain higher level qualifications at a distance. These Universities were the University of London, the Royal University of Ireland and the University of St. Andrews.

In the USA a number of developments led the way for the adoption of correspondence study by the extension departments of American universities. As early as in 1874 the Illinois Wesleyan University began to offer 8 undergraduate and graduate courses which could be pursued in absentia. This programme was discontinued in 1910. In 1883 the Correspondence University at Itcha, New York, was founded with teachers from various universities with the objective of providing correspondence courses to students unable to attend regular institutions. Although acclaimed at that time, the venture was not successful. In 1883 Chautauqua was permitted by the New York State Legislature to offer correspondence study programme leading to Bachelor of Divinity and Bachelor of Arts. Later the programme was closed. William Harper, the father of American distance education, offered instruction in Hebrew by mail in the 1880s. In 1891 Thomas Foster, the editor of Mining Herald, a daily newspaper in the mining district of eastern Pennsylvania, taught through his newspaper mining and methods of preventing mine accidents. This experiment paved the way for preparation of many correspondence courses in various fields. In fact, these constitute the base for the beginning of the International Correspondence Schools in Pennsylvania and their subsidiaries and offshoots.

The mother of American correspondence study was Anna Eliot Ticknor, daughter of a Harvard University professor, who founded and ran the Boston-based Society to encourage study at home from 1873 until her death in 1897. The idea of exchanging letters between teacher and student originated with her and monthly correspondence with guided readings and frequent tests formed a vital part of the organization's personalized instruction. Although the curriculum reflected the "classical orientation", it is interesting that most of her students were women, a clientele then only beginning to demand access to higher education.

The wondrous developments of technology during the Industrial Revolution brought about, for the first time in history, the possibility of distance education. These developments were particularly important in transport and communication. It was no coincidence, writes Peters (1973), that the first trains, the first postal systems and the first correspondence courses commenced at the same time because they are intrinsically linked.

By the end of nineteenth century correspondence education was widely practiced and accepted to a greater or lesser degree as a valid means of studying. This acceptance paved the way for developments in the twentieth century. The twentieth century experienced increased interest in correspondence education as a means of equalizing educational opportunities, providing education to a scattered population over vast distance, offering education to deprived and disadvantaged sections of society.

In early years of the 20thcentury in Australia, Canada, New Zealand correspondence education was adopted by national and state governments as a means of extending the school system to those who would otherwise be deprived. The Australian Correspondence school system originated in 1914. The founding of Queensland University in 1909 spread correspondence education in Australia.

Along with the growth of correspondence education, bodies designed to accredit and regularize the activities of correspondence schools and colleges came to be established. Prominent among these were the US National University Extension Association (1915), the US National Home Study Council (1926), and the Association of British Correspondence Colleges (1955).

During the 1920s the Soviet Union began to use correspondence education. A Central Institute for Correspondence Education was established in 1927. In 1930s correspondence education became an organic part of the Soviet Public Education System. Peters (1973) in his survey of distance teaching at university level in early 1960s identified eleven distance-teaching universities in the USSR. About 40 per cent of all university enrolled students were in distance universities. In 1979 there were 14 distance-teaching universities and over 100-evening learning centres and a large number of people qualified in undergraduate and postgraduate courses while continuing in their employment. The introduction of correspondence education in the Indian University System in 1960s was largely influenced by the Soviet correspondence education.

Up to the 1960s the large scale distance teaching organizations had been with very few exceptions - private correspondence schools. The beginning of 1960s and 1970s saw publicly supported and established schools and universities becoming more and more important and significant. A pioneer in this respect is the University of South Africa, which emerged as a development of the University of Good Hope, founded in 1873 as an examining body based on the model of the University of London. It started teaching at a distance in 1946. The University of South Africa was established as a distance teaching university through governmental decree of 1962.

In the recent decades distance education improved quantitatively and qualitatively. Keegan (1986) attributed this to:

- development of new communications technology
- growing sophistication in the use of print materials
- improved design of instructional materials
- improved provision of support services for students studying at a distance
- Establishment of the British Open University in 1969 and the subsequent foundation of similar structures both in developed and developing countries.

Inspite of its increasing validity, reliability and utility, distance education has not gained full recognition and wholehearted support of many academics, mostly from the conventional system.

The comments of Perry (1976), the first Vice-Chancellor of the British Open University, on the emergence of the Open University reflect this situation:

> "The advent of the Open University added a much needed academic respectability to distance education, lending moral support and confidence to teaching staff and administrators of the courses. It is seen and is commended by the academic world. The quality of the students, the quality of the exams – they are all recognized by the academics in other universities. But emotionally, many of them don't accept it at all.... Emotionally there still is a strong feeling that on campus teaching in the face-to-face situation is the only way of actually teaching and that this is the vital thing in order to train scholars for the future. It may take decades rather than years to overcome this emotional reaction. You have to remember, I suppose, that every advance in education has been resisted for years and years. When we tried to introduce universal primary education, people argued that losing child labour out of coal mines would cause economic unrest. The same sort of people objected to universal secondary education because it was going to over educate the working classes who ought to be kept in their place and learn a trade. I suppose the same reaction occurs to the

idea of universal tertiary education and of certainly the opportunity for it".

It is not possible to paint an accurate picture of the current status of distance education on a worldwide basis, for a number of reasons. First, as already mentioned, there is such a wide range of types and levels of provision, covering all sectors of education, both private and public, from school level to postgraduate study, and for technical, vocational, and professional training. Hence responsibility for distance education provision, even in a single country, may be spread over a whole range of different organizations, ministries, and departments. Secondly, the published material available on distance education provision in many countries is very patchy, and seems to be inversely proportional to the number of students involved.

Definition of Distance Education

There are a number of problems in trying to define distance education. The first problem is with the word 'distance'. It has different connotations. It is not restricted to the idea of mere physical distance from the location of teaching. Initially distance methods may have developed in some countries because of students' difficulties in travelling to distant conventional institutions. Now 'distance' in geographical sense is not a major necessary defining characteristic of distance education. The most meaningful use of the term 'distance' is that proposed by Moore in the expression 'transactional distance'. Transactional distance is the gap of understanding and communication between the teachers and learners caused by geographical distance that must be bridged through distinctive procedures in instructional design and the facilitation of interaction.

The second problem experienced in defining distance education lies in great diversity of practices, systems and projects that are commonly covered by the term. A rapid evolution of methods and structures in the recent past contributed greatly to the diversity in the field of distance education. The many forms of distance education existing today have evolved from a wide variety of different sources. The distance teaching universities established in recent decades promoted comprehensive image of distance education. All these factors contribute to the difficulty of defining distance education. Inspite of problems, distance education has been variously defined. There is yet no agreement on a single definition. In recent years rich contribution to the discussion of distance education has been made by Charles Wedemeyer, Michael Moore, Rumble, Otto

Peters, Borje Holmberg, John Baath, David Stewart, Hillary Perraton and Desmand Keegan.

There are some educators who feel that terminology is unimportant and that there is little need to divert resources for analysis. "Let us all do more of it without worrying too much about what it is".

Though it is easier to devise a definition than to accept someone else's, we will not be tempted to do it. We will highlight those elements which are essential to any definition. We give below four definitions which will cover all the important elements to any definition of distance education.

> "The term 'distance education' covers the various forms of study at all levels which are not under the continuous, immediate supervision of tutors present with their students in lecture rooms or on the same premises, but which nevertheless, benefit from the planning, guidance and tuition of a tutorial organisation".
>
> — Holmberg (1977)

> "Distance teaching education is a method of imparting knowledge, skills and attitudes which is rationalised by the application of division of labour and organisation principles as well as by the extensive use of technical media, especially for the purpose of reproducing high quality teaching material which makes it possible to instruct great numbers of students at the same time wherever they live. It is an industrialized form of teaching and learning".
>
> — Peters (1973)

> "Distance education is a systematically organised form of self-study in which student counselling, the presentation of learning material and the securing and supervising of students' success is carried out by a team of teachers, each of whom has responsibilities. It is made possible by means of media which can cover long distances. The opposite of distance education is direct education or face-to-face education: a type of education that takes place with direct contact between lecturers and students".
>
> — Dohmen (1967)

> Distance teaching may be defined as the family of instructional methods in which the teaching behaviours are executed apart from the learning behaviours including those that in a contiguous situation would be performed in the learner's presence, so that communication between the teacher and the learner must be facilitated by print, electronic, mechanical or other devices".
>
> —Moore (1973)

A Comprehensive Definition of Distance Education

A comprehensive and general definition of distance education was first proposed by Keegan in 1980 and subsequently modified by him in 1986. Keegan (1986) attempted a synthesis of most of the definitions by identifying the following seven defining elements of a distance education:

- The quasi-permanent separation of teacher and learner throughout the length of the learning process.
- The influence of an educational organization both in the planning and preparation of learning materials and in the provision of student support services.
- The use of technical media, print, audio, video or computer, to unite teacher and learner and carry the content of the course.
- The provision of two-way communication so that the student may benefit from or even initiate dialogue.
- The quasi-permanent absence of the learning group throughout the length of the learning process so that people usually taught as individuals and not in groups, with the possibility of occasional meetings, either for face-to-face or by electronic means, both for didactic and socialization purposes.
- The privatization of institutional learning.
- The presence of more industrialized features than in conventional oral education.

The definition of Keegan seeks to take up the middle ground "between the extremes of defining distance education so narrowly that it becomes an abstraction which does not correspond to existing reality, or so broadly that it becomes meaningless as the basis for analysis and the development of grounded theory". Keegan excludes from his concept of distance education the following:

- The use of printed, audio-based, video-based and computer-based learning materials in classroom lectures, theatres, seminars, tutorial and laboratory sessions for on-campus programmes.
- The use of printed, audio-based, video-based learning material and computers in private study.

Terminological Variety

There are many terms similar to 'distance education'. Some of such terms are:

- Distance teaching

- Distance learning
- Distance teaching and learning
- Open learning
- Flexible learning
- Distributed learning
- Open distance learning
- Blended learning
- E-learning
- Mobile learning (M-learning)
- Self-managed learning
- Supported self-study
- Independent study

Let us clarify the meanings of some of these terms and the differences between them.

Distance Teaching and Learning: Distance education encompasses distance teaching and distance learning processes. The three terms are used synonymously. A noted distance educator summed up the pros and cons of the term 'distance education':

> "I do not like the term 'distance education'. It seems to put a undue emphasis on the distance between the teacher and the learner. But I cannot think of a better name for a multimedia educational process in which the teacher and the students never meet in the face-to-face situation. 'Distance teaching' seems too teacher oriented and 'distance learning' too student-based. Distance education combines the two. So, in the absence of a better name for the process, I shall use it when appropriate".

Open Learning: Open learning is a different concept from that of distance education. In 1975 the concept which had emerged during the 1950's and 1960's was described in MacKenzie et al's UNESCO book, *Open Learning: Systems and Problems in Post-Secondary Education* as an "imprecise phrase to which a range of meanings can be, and is attached. It eludes definition. But as an inscription to be carried, in a procession on a banner, gathering adherents and enthusiasms, it has great potential".

Someone else defined open learning system as "one in which the restrictions placed on students are under constant review and removed wherever possible. It incorporates the widest range of teaching strategies, in particular those using independent and individualized learning". In 1984 UK Manpower Services Commission expressed that "open learning arrangements enable people to learn at the time and place which satisfy their circumstances and requirements". The emphasis is on opening up opportunities by overcoming barriers that result from geographical isolation, personal or work commitments or conventional course structures which have often prevented people gaining access to the training they need". In 1988 Lewis and MacDonald gave the following definition which is now widely accepted:

"Open learning describes ways of helping individuals to take responsibilities for their own learning. Learners may, for example, choose:

- What they learn
- How they learn
- Where they learn
- Why they learn
- How quickly they learn
- Who to turn to for help
- Whether, when and where to have their learning assessed".

This indicates a range of freedoms, open learning can make possible for students. Within this territory, sits distance learning which enables education to be accessed across geographical distance, by students who need not be in regular face to face contact with their tutors. The freedoms made possible by open provision can be grouped under two main headings: (a) choices in access (time, place and pace in the above definition) and (b) choices within the curriculum itself (the other points in the list). The distance learning subset of open learning concentrates on the former.

Distance education and open learning are not totally different. The former stresses the means by which education is achieved, the latter the objectives and character of the educational process.

As Rumble stated open learning system is not separate from distance education as a method of education. Distance education systems may be either closed or open in relation to the criteria for openness. But distance systems tend towards openness in so far as they are 'time free' and 'space free'. Many open learning systems are closed in relation to the criteria for openness.

As Lewis (1985) pointed out "openness is relative: provision is more or less open".

Flexible Learning: Flexible learning is an umbrella term covering both open and distance learning. This implies a system that is more than just the use of learning packages. Degree of flexibility depends very much on the institution, course, tutor, and the individual. A flexible learning system is one which offers a range of freedoms designed to meet the needs of the individual.

Key Features of Flexible Learning System	
Access to Learning	*Choices within the Course*
Choice of location – learner chooses where to study	Choice of modules, course offers many possible destinations
Choice of time of day and day of week	Choice of mode of study, learner can use several media
Entry to course at any time of year	Negotiate course content, learner negotiates course content
Prior learning in place of entry qualifications, anyone can study	Choice of method of assessment, learner is involved in assessing progress
Ability to work at own pace, learner sets the pace	Credit accumulation and transfer
Ability to roll-on roll-off course, learner can set own completion date	Access to tutor support when required
Payment by installment	Learner negotiates programme of study
Resource centres open outside hours	Learner selects from support options

Open Distance Learning: In recent years, some new terms are in currency: 'open and distance learning', 'open distance learning', 'open learning and distance education' etc. Rumble's recent book titled *'The Cost and Economics of Open and Distance Learning"* Keith Harry's latest edited collection '*Higher Education through Open and Distance learning*', International Council for Distance Education is now termed 'International Council for Open and Distance Education'. In the early 1990s the European Commission introduced the term 'open distance learning' for its policies and programmes in the broad field. Though the expression has now wide international currency, it is confusing and misleading people about the educational purposes aimed at. As indicated earlier, 'open learning' stand for the general aim of opening up educational opportunities more freely and widely. Openness has many dimensions but only a few pursued. Distance education on the other hand, is one method of pursuing some dimensions of openness. A simple way to summarise scholarly reflection on these terms is "to say that open learning may or may not involve distance education whereas distance education may or may not contribute to open learning".

Blended Learning: Blended learning is often defined as the combination of face-to-face and online learning. It is viewed as an opportunity to redesign the way that courses are developed, scheduled and delivered in higher education through a combination of physical and virtual instruction "bricks and clicks". The goal of these redesigned courses is to join the best features of in-class teaching with the best faculties of online learning to promote active, self-directed learning opportunities for students with added flexibility. Several research students have demonstrated that the blended learning designs contribute to improved learning outcomes for students. Blended learning courses have higher success rates and lower withdrawal rates.

E-Learning: The term e-learning came into regular use around 2000. It is commonly used but does not have common definition. It has different meaning to different people. It is frequently used interchangeably with term such as online learning, virtual learning, distributed learning, web-based learning. Despite their unique attributes each of these term fundamentals refers to educational processes that utilize information and communication technology to mediate asynchronous as well as synchronous learning and teaching activities.

Forces driving the growth and development of e-learning include:

- The increasing accessibility as well as the decreasing costs of ICTSs
- The capacity of ICTs to support and enrich conventional educational practices through resource-based learning and synchronous and asynchronous communication.
- The need for flexibility in access to learning opportunities from distributed venues such as the home, workplace, community centre and the conventional educational institution.
- The demand from isolated and independent learners for more equitable access to educational opportunities and services.
- The belief and expectation that online learning will reduce costs and increases productivity and institutional efficiency.

In e-learning method several kinds of tools are used apart from internet, intranet and network tools such as Blogging Tools, E-Mail, News Group, Bulletin Boards, Web Forms, Polling, Wikis, White Board, Course Management System, Internet Technology, Instant Messaging, Online Discussion, etc.

Mobile Learning: Mobile learning, or m-learning, is a personal, spontaneous, "anytime and anywhere" way to learn and to access educational tools and material that enlarges access to education for all. It reinforces learners' sense of ownership of the learning experience, offering them flexibility in how, when and where they learn.

In developing countries, mobile technologies potentially deliver education without dependence on an extensive traditional communications infrastructure.

Although m-learning experience remains limited, it is becoming a credible, cost-effective component of blended open and distance learning provisions, adaptable to an institution's needs and situation.

M-learning devices are light weights and handheld, including:

- Personal Digital Assistants and Palmtop or Handheld Computers
- Mobile Phones also called Cell Phones or Hand Phones.

M-learning has developed mainly in Europe, America and in parts of Asia. M-learning has been shaped by the specific ideas of teaching and learning; specific relations between teacher, student and subject and the specific roles for different educational institutions, found in the societies and institutions it has evolved.

M-learning applications include:

(a) teaching and learning
(b) transmitting content
(c) shared discussion
(d) independent study skills and
(e) workplace education

Distributed Learning: Distributed Learning is a broader term that is associated with face-to-face instructions. It incorporates some form of technology based learning experiences, either inside or outside the classroom. In other words, students do not need to be at a distance from their instruction to benefit from distributed learning. Many distributed learning experiences may involve only resources that are at distance, or that occurs at a different time or place than the conventional class meeting.

One of the earliest definitions of distributed learning was offered by Saltzberg and Polyson (1995):

> "Distributed learning is not just a new term to replace the other distance learning. Rather, it comes from the concept of distributed resources. It is an instructional model that allows instructor, students and content to be located in different, non centralised locations so that instruction and learning occurs independent of place and time. The distributed learning model can be used in combination with traditional classroom based courses, with traditional distance learning courses, or it can be used to create wholly virtual classrooms."

Independent Study: This term 'independent study' was chosen in the mid-1960s by university administrators to describe their correspondence courses and to distinguish them from the private, for-profit schools. There are more than 150 universities providing such courses in the USA. The content of courses tends to be more academic than vocational and there will be more interaction between instructors and students. In addition to the printed study materials, university independent study courses are more likely to include other technologies, such as video tapes, television broadcasts, CD ROMs and use of Internet. There is a great variety in the independent study courses available. Offerings include degree programmes at the associate, bachelor or masters levels, as well as certificate programmes and non-credit courses. Many universities allow their on campus students to take their independent courses as a way to solving class scheduling problems. Usually no distinction is made in transcripts between the grades awarded for courses taken in class and courses taken by independent study. Some universities provide high school courses through independent study. University of Nebraska Lincoln has been offering such courses since 1929. It currently offers 160 courses in 15 subject areas. The American Association of Collegiate Independent Study is a professional association of administrators and academics in independent study.

Components of Distance Education System

According to Rumble (1986), the components of a distance education system are:

- Curriculum planning,
- Materials development, production storage, and delivery,
- Student recruitment, admission and counseling,
- Organizations of study of facilities and support services,
- Tutoring, assessment and examination of students,
- Monitoring of student progress,
- General and specialist administration and management, and
- Research and evaluation.

The range of media used in distance education system provides an added dimension to the components.

UNESCO's Publication (2002) *Open and Distance Learning: Trends, Policy and Strategy Considerations* indicate, eight components of all distance education systems:

- Mission
- Courses and curricula

- Teaching strategies and techniques
- Learning materials and resources
- Communication
- Support delivered locally
- Student and staff management
- Management and administration

Support to Distance Education

Different reasons are given by different theorists and practitioners for the strong support to distance education by governments, the private sector and individual students. Bates (2005) gave the following reasons:

- Lifelong learning
- Social equity and access
- Better education
- Cost effectiveness
- Geography
- Commercialization of education

Rumble (1986) highlighted the following underlying factors that led to the adoption of distance education as an instrument of national educational policy:

- Egalitarianism
- Modernization theories
- Rural development
- Community education
- Need for training
- Economy
- Totalitarianism

Use of Distance Education

Distance education has a valid and important role to play in national education systems and can serve a variety of needs; that it can be a profitable field of activity for private enterprise; and that it can be used by large companies as a means of training their employees. Because of flexibility, distance education is one of the most important means of providing for the education of adult both for ongoing vocational and professional training in non-vocational fields.

Public and private educational institutional, governments have introduced distance education provision in order to:

- increase access to learning and training opportunities,
- provide increased opportunities for updating, retraining and personal enrichment,
- improve cost-effectiveness of educational resources,
- support the quality and variety of existing educational structures, and
- enhance and consolidate capacity

In the light of the experiences of the past several years, there is today recognition of other related benefits. Some these are:

- balancing inequalities between age groups,
- extending geographical access to education
- delivering educational campaigns and other education for large audiences
- providing speedy and efficient training for key target groups,
- expanding the capacity of education in new and multidisciplinary subject areas,
- offering the combination of education with work and family life,
- developing multiple competencies through recurrent and continuing education,
- enhancing the international dimensions of education experiences, and
- improving the quality of existing educational services.

Distance education is by no means the panacea for national educational problem that some of its supporters would like to believe. However, the weight of available evidence indicates in a fairly clear that in both developed and developing countries – distance methods can make an original and effective contribution to individual, societal and development goals.

2

Theoretical Basis of Distance Education

The need for a theoretical basis for distance education has been stressed by researchers, scholars, and practitioners. Delling (1975), a reputed historian of distance education, stated that though distance education existed for about hundred years, it was only during the last few years that the provision of distance education began to rely on theory. Delling wrote: "We need distance education theory to interpret experiences to guide systematic research, to develop distance education, to train the distance educators and finally to elucidate the problems of distance education in discussion with face to face educators". Charles Wedemeyer (1987) felt that distance education failed to develop a theory related to the mainstream of educational thought and practice. Keegan (1986) urged for a firmly based theory of distance education which can provide the touchstone against which decisions—political, financial, educational and social, can be taken with confidence.

Although forms of distance education existed since many decades and attempts at theoretical explanations of distance education had been undertaken by leading scholars in the field, the need for a theory base of distance education was still largely unfulfilled in the 1970s (Simonson, Samaldino, Albright and Zvacek, 2009). Holmberg (1985) stated that further theoretical considerations would contribute results that would give distance educators a firmly based theory, a touchstone against which decisions could be made with confidence. Keegan (1998) implied the continued need for a theory of distance education when he lamented the task of it: "Lack of accepted theory has weakened distance education: there has been a lack of identity, a sense of belonging to the periphery and the lack of a touchstone against which decisions of methods, on media, on financing, on student support, when they have to be made, can be made with confidence".

Some writers and practitioners expressed doubts about the possibility of a theory of distance education. Rumble (1986) stated categorically that the "search for a firmly based theory of distance education which is comprehensive in nature is misconceived". Perraton (2000) found it "native to seek a single theory of distance education but it is possible to make theoretical statements using the term 'the theory' in a strict and narrow sense". Others admitted that distance education is developing its own body of theory, although it is currently ill-defined and illusive.

Inspite of several doubts and apprehensions about the feasibility and possibility of a sound theory of distance education, theoretical approaches have been attempted to date. Some of them are the best available in the literature. These theoretical positions and approaches are classified under the following three kinds by Keegan in his landmark work *The Foundations of Distance Education.*

- *Theories of Autonomy and Independence:* These contributions come mainly from the late 1960s and early 1970s and the major representatives are Manfred Delling (FRG), Charles A Wedemeyer (USA) and Michael G Moore (USA)
- *Theory of Industrialization of Teaching:* Otto Peter's work in the Federal Republic of Germany comprised comparative studies throughout the 1960s and theoretical formulation in the early 1970s.
- *Theories of Interaction and Communication:* More contemporary views from Borje Holmberg (Sweden/Federal Republic of Germany), John A Baath (Sweden), David Sewart (UK), Kevin C Smith (Australia), and John S Daniel (UK).
- A fourth group seeks to explain distance education in a synthesis of existing theories of communication and diffusion.

Theories of Autonomy and Independence

Delling in 1975 offered the following:

> "Distance education (Fernunterricht) is a planned and systematic activity which comprises the choice, didactic preparation and presentation of teaching materials as well as the supervision and support of student learning and which is achieved by bridging the physical distance between student and teacher by means of at least one appropriate technical medium".

For Delling distance education is a multi-dimensional system of learning and communication process with the aid of an artificial signal carrier. He mentions eight dimensions of distance education: learner, society, helping organisation, learning objective, commitment to be learned, result of learning, distance and signal carrier. He excludes teaching from the eight dimension of the system. Feedback and two-way communications are central. He gives low position to the teacher and the educational organisation and focuses on the autonomy and independence of the learner.

Wedemeyer (1971) 'evolved a theory of 'independent study'. He used the term 'independent study' to described distance education at university level and provided this definition:

> "Independent learning' is that learning, that changed behaviour, that results from activities carried on by learners in space and time, learners whose environment in different from that of the school, learners who may be guided by teachers but who are not dependent upon them, learners who accept degrees of freedom and responsibility in initiating and carrying out the activities that lead to learning".

Wedemeyer's concept of independent study consists of two forms of education: independent study for the internal student and independent study for the external student. He framed a conceptual structure comprising the following ten features of the system:

- The system should be capable of operation at any place where there are students – or even only one student—whether or not there are teachers at the same place at the same time
- The system should place greater responsibility for learning on the student.
- The system should free faculty members from custodial type duties so that more time can be given to truly educational tasks.
- The system should offer students and adults wider choices (more opportunities) in courses, formats, methodologies.
- The system should use, as appropriate all the teaching media and methods that have been proved effective.
- The system should mix and combine media and methods so that each subject or unit within a subject is taught in the best way known.
- The system should cause the redesign and development of courses to fit into an 'articulated media programme'.

- The system should preserve and enhance opportunities for adaptation to individual differences.
- The system should evaluate student achievement simply, not by raising barriers concerned with the place the student studies, the rate at which he studies, the method by which he studies or the sequence within which he studies.
- The system should permit students to start, stop and learn at their own pace.

Formulated in the early 1970s, Moore's theory of distance education which he calls 'independent study' is a classification method for distance education programmes. It examines two variables in educational programmes: the amount of learner autonomy and the distance between teacher and learner. Transactional distance connotes the interplay among environment, individuals and the patterns of behaviours in a situation. Moore (1977) states that the theory of transactional distance is typology of all education programmes having this distinguishing characteristic of separation of teacher and learner. Transactional distance is relative rather than absolute, and describes the full range of all possible degrees of structure, dialogue, and autonomy in environments that have the special characteristic of teacher and student being spatially separated from one another.

For Moore, distance education is composed of two elements, each of which can be measured. First is the provision of two-way communication (dialog). Some systems or programmes offer two way communications. Second is the extent to which programmes are responsible to the needs of the individual learner (structure). Some programmes are very structured, while others are very responsive to the needs and goals of the individual student.

In the second part of his theory Moore addresses learners' autonomy. He notes that in traditional settings, learners are dependent on teachers for guidance. In most programmes the teacher is active and the student is passive. In distance education, there is a gap between teacher and student and the student must accept a high degree of responsibility for the learning programme.

Moore classifies distance education programmes as 'autonomous' (learner determined) or 'non autonomous' (teacher determined).

Wedemeyer proposed separating teaching from learning as a way of breaking education's space-time barriers. He suggested six characteristics of independent study systems:

- The student and teacher are separated
- The normal process of teaching and learning are carried out in writing or through some other medium.
- Teaching is individualized.
- Learning taken place through the student's activity
- Learning is made convenient for the student in his or her own environment.
- The learner takes responsibility for the pace of his or her own progress with freedom to start and stop at any time.

Wedemeyer (1987) noted four elements of every teaching/learning situation: a teacher, a learner or learners, a communication system or mode, and something to be taught or learned. He proposed a reorganization of these elements that would accommodate physical space and allow greater learner freedom. Key to the success of distance education, Wedemeyer believed, was the development of the relationship between student and teacher.

Wedemyer tried to promote non-traditional education programmes in the highly structured USA university system. His propositions and beliefs are reflected in his book *'Learning at the Back Door'*. As Keegan said "his personal dedication, generosity and liberal vision' contributed much to the growth of a consensus among distance educators throughout the world and influenced many writers".

Michael Moore transformed Wedemeyer's ideas into insightful and analytical model of independent study.

Theory of Industrialization

Otto Peters (1973) did pioneering work by undertaking an analytical and comparative survey of distance education institutions at further level throughout the world. From his surveys Peters developed a theoretical structure for distance education. He found similarities between industrial production process and the teaching/learning process in distance education. Analysis of industrial production process led him to consider distance education as the industrial form of teaching and learning. Peters presented a comparison of distance teaching and the industrial production of goods under the heads: rationalization, division of labour, mechanization, assembly lines, mass production, preparatory work, formalization, standardization, functional change, objectification, concentration, centralization, planning, organization and scientific control methods.

Peters concluded that for distance teaching to become effective, the principle of the division of labour is a constituent element of distance teaching. The teaching process in his theory of industrialization is generally restructured through increasing mechanization and automation. He noted that:

- the development of distance study courses is just as important as the preparatory work – taking place prior to the production process.
- the effectiveness of the teaching process particularly depends on planning and organization.
- courses must be formalized and expectations of students must be standardized.
- the teaching process is largely objectified.
- the function of academics teaching at a distance has changed considerably vis-a-vis university teachers in conventional teaching.
- distance study can only be economical with a concentration of the available resources and a centralized administration.

A theory of industrialization of teaching had disadvantages, but in any exploration of teaching, the industrial structured characteristic of distance teaching need to be taken into account in decision making.

Theories of Interaction and Communication

Among the writers who emphasized interaction and communication in distance education, the prominent ones are John A. Baath, Holmberg, Daniel, Sewart and K.C. Smith.

Baath (1980) made an important theoretical contribution by developing the concept of two-way communication as a major defining feature of distance education systems. He examined the applicability of teaching models of Skinner, Rothkopf, Ausubel, Egan, Bruner, Rogers and Gagne to correspondence education (a subset of distance education) and found the functions of two-way communication in correspondence education in the light of each of the specified teaching models. Baath studied:

- the relationship of submission density (frequency of assignment submission during a course and a two way communication)
- the replacement of tutor marked assignments by self-assessment questions, and

- the introduction of computer-marked assignments as a form of two way communication

Baath's theoretical contributions resulted from his experiences in Sweden. He expressed how his own experience led to his construction:

> 'When writing correspondence course materials, I was struck by the idea that it was possible to provide some kind of two-way communication within the material, by means of exercises, questions or self-check tests with detailed model or specimen answers. Could such two-way communication, to any considerable extent, replace the postal two-way communication induced by assignments for submission".

Personal experience and theoretical investigation together led Baath to place two way communications as centre to the distance education process and the distance tutors as central to his concept.

Holmberg (1995) significantly broadened his theory of distance education. His new comprehensive theory is divided into eight parts. This expanded theory encompasses the theory just stated previously, plus these additions:

- Distance education serves individual learners who cannot or do not want to make use of face-to-face teaching. These learners are very heterogeneous.
- Distance education means learners no longer have to be bounded by decisions made by others about place of study, division of the year into study terms and vacations, timetables and entry requirements. Distance education thus promotes students' freed of choice and independence.
- Society benefits from distance education, on the one hand, from the liberal study opportunities it affords individual learners, and on the other hand, from the professional/occupational training it provides.
- Distance education is in instrument for recurrent and lifelong learning for free access to learning opportunities and equity.
- All learning concerned with acquisition of cognitive knowledge and cognitive skills as well as effective learning and some psychomotor learning are effectively provided by distance education.
- Distance education is based on deep learning as an individual activity. Learning is guided and supported by noncontiguous

means. Teaching and learning rely on mediated communication, usually based on pre-produced courses.

- Distance education is open to behaviourist, cognitive, constructivist and other models of learning. It has an element of industrialization with division of labour, use of mechanical devices, electronic data processing and mass communication usually based on pre-produced courses.
- Personal relations, study pleasure, and empathy between students and those supporting them are central to learning in distance education. Feeling of empathy and belonging promote students' motivation to learn and influence the learning favourably. Such feelings are conveyed by students being engaged in decision making; by lucid, problem oriented conversations like presentations of learning matter which may be anchored in existing knowledge; by friendly, non- contiguous interaction between students, tutors counselors, and others supporting them; and by liberal organizational or administrative structures and processes.

Holmberg (1986) characterizes distance study as self-study. The student gets benefited from a course developed for him and also through interaction with his tutors and other staff of a supporting organization. The relationship between the supporting organization and the student is described as a guided didactic conversation (GDC). This might be presented diagrammatically and schematically as follows.

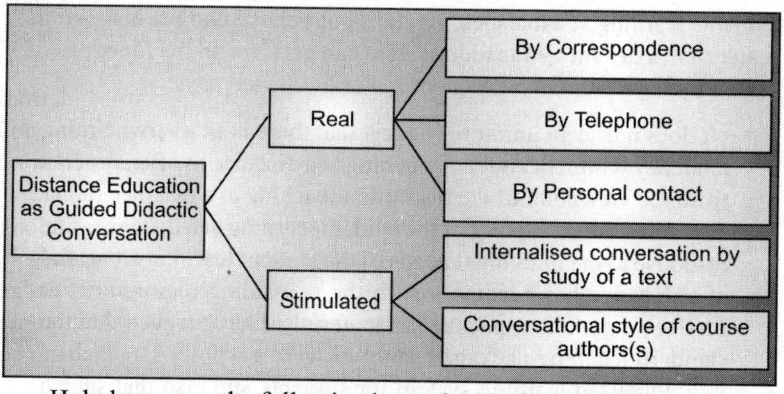

Holmberg gave the following bases for his framework:

- that feelings of personal relation between teaching and learning parties which promotes study pleasure and motivation.

- that such feelings can be fostered by well developed self-instructional material and suitable two way communication at a distance.
- that intellectual pleasure and study motivation are favourable to the attainment of study goals and the use of proper study processes and methods.
- that the atmosphere, language and conventions of friendly conversation favour feelings of personal relation according to first postulate.

According to John Daniel, a former Vice-Chancellor of the British Open University, emergence of distance education according to him is the result of the combination of three sources: (a) long tradition of independent study (b) recent developments in the teaching of education and (c) new theoretical interest in open learning. The first of these elements has produced new educational enterprises which teach at a distance. Distance systems comprise, according to Daniel, activities in which the student works alone and activities which bring him into contact with other people. The first group activities he calls independent activities and the second interactive. Distance education system should achieve synthesis between independence and interaction.

David Sewart (1983) is a former Director of Regional Academic Services at the British Open University. He was managerially responsible for the provision of support services to students. His theoretical approach to distance education can be summed as a continuity of concern for students learning at a distance. He does not believe that the instructional material in a distance education system can perform all the functions of a class room teacher. On package of material, Sewart says:

> "It does not seem unfair to suggest that there is an overwhelming tendency within the field of teaching at a distance to offer systems from the viewpoint of the institution teaching at a distance rather than from the view point of the student learning at a distance. The response to the individual needs of the student learning alone and at a distance has become lost in the overriding requirement to produce a grandiose package of materials. I have argued that the standard teaching package cannot provide a wholly satisfactory individualised learning system for students and also that such a package suffers from a tendency towards tight curriculum control. It is only the introduction of human element, capable of adapting

to the great variety of student needs, which can counteract this sort of bias".

Sewart demands an interactive mode in distance systems which can hardly be supplied by the learning materials. He strongly feels that advice and support for distance student poses almost infinitely variable problems and this creates the need for an advisory and supportive role of a distance institution in addition to the provision of a teaching package. He strongly holds that it is the continuity of the institution's concern for quality of support in a distance system that has been the UKOU's success in solving the critical problems of distance system such as the avoidance of avoidable dropouts.

Australian integrated mode of teaching comprises face-to-face teaching and distance teaching by the full time faculty of the Universities. K.C. Smith (1987), who greatly contributed for the development of distance education in Australia, pleads for the division of work of university faculty equally between on-campus and off-campus students. The external students enroll in the same courses, take the same examinations and are awarded the same degrees as the conventional ones.

Smith's position is based on the following ideas:

- External teaching should not be done by part-time tutors but by the full-time university faculty.
- By being part of a normal university a distance system remains in the educational mainstream.
- A university has only a small pool of outstanding staff; external students should be in contact with them, not with what he calls 'part-time recruits'.
- A university is a community of scholars and all distance students must become part of this community by attending compulsory residential schools.
- Concentration on the learning package can lead to a dehumanizing of the learning process, as this is a social experience.
- Distance education must not depend solely on correspondence methods. Some degree of interaction not only with materials but also with other students and the teachers are essential.

Smith suggests the following advantages of integrated mode:

- *Legitimacy:* internal and external studies are legitimate activities of universities.
- *Mainstream Activity:* distance teaching should be undertaken

by full-time academic staff as part of their normal teaching responsibilities so that it will benefit from the scholarship, resource allocation, and status.

- *Commitment:* commitment is likely if the whole process remains the responsibility of the academic staff and is not divided.
- *Parity:* Parity of esteem for degrees can best be achieved if the same staff of the university teach and evaluate both kinds of students.
- *Interaction:* group discussions among staff and students and between students themselves are beneficial.
- *Variety:* variety of teaching methods is recommended because of the diversity of students.
- *Independence/Pacing:* Pacing of students is a feature of successful systems.
- *Communication:* a distance system requires a strong administration.

A critique of Smith's position is that he frequently puts forward the particular solutions of his own institution as normative for other institutions. The Australian integrated mode is of certain interest as a model for a small system with less number of students. As Keegan felt Smith's contribution is a refreshing one and that it would be too much to say that Smiths' writings contain a theory of distance education; rather they present a service of heartfelt beliefs on how external students should be administered.

A Synthesis of Existing Theories-Hilary Perraton

Perraton's theory of distance education (2000) is composed of elements from existing theories of communication and diffusion, as well as philosophies of education. It is expressed in the form of 14 statements, or hypotheses. The first five of these statements concern the way distance teaching can be used to maximize education:

- You can use any medium to teach anything.
- Distance teaching can break the integuments of fixed staffing ratios that limited the expansion of education when teacher and student had to be in the same place at the same time.
- There are circumstances under which distance teaching can be cheaper than orthodox education, whether measured in terms of audience reached or of learning.
- The economies achievable by distance education are functions

of the level of education, size of audience, choice of media, and sophistication of production.

- Distance teaching can reach audiences who would not be reached by ordinary means.

The following four statements address the need to increase dialog:

- It is possible to organize distance teaching in such a way that there is dialog.
- Where a tutor meets distance students face-to-face, the tutor's role is changed from that of a communicator of information to that of a facilitator of learning.
- Group discussion is an effective method of learning when distance teaching is used to bring relevant information to the group.
- In most communities, resources are available that can be used to support distance learning to its educational and economic advantage.

The final five statements deal with method:

- A multimedia programme is likely to be more effective than one that relies on a single medium.
- A systems approach is helpful in planning distance education.
- Feedback is a necessary part of a distance learning system.
- To be effective, distance teaching materials should ensure that students undertake frequent and regular activities over and above reading, watching, or listening.
- In choosing between media, the key decision on which the rest depend concerns the use of face-to-face learning.

Keegan (1996) suggested that the theoretician had to answer three questions before developing a theory of distance education:

1. Is distance education an educational activity?
2. Is distance education a form of conventional education?
3. Is distance education possible, or is it a contradiction in terms?

Central to Keegan's concept of distance education is the separation of the teaching acts in time and place from the learning acts. Successful distance education, he believes, requires the reintegration of the two acts:

- The inter subjectivity of teaching and learner, in which learning from teaching occurs, has to be artificially re-created. Over space and time, a distance system seeks to reconstruct the moment in which the teaching/iearning interaction occurs. The linking of learning materials to learning is central to this process.

- Reintegration of the act of teaching at a distance is attempted in two ways. First learning materials, both printed and non-print, redesigned to achieve as many of the characteristics of interpersonal communication as possible. Second, when courses are presented, reintegration of the teaching act is attempted by a variety of techniques, including communication by correspondence, telephone tutorial, online computer communication, comments on assignments by tutors or computers, and teleconferences.

The process of reintegrating the act of teaching in distance education, results in at least five changes to normal structures of oral, group-based education:

1. The industrialization of teaching .
2. The privatization of institutional learning
3. Change of administrative structure
4. Different plant and buildings
5. Change of costing structures

Keegan offers three hypotheses drawn from his theoretical framework:

1. Distance students have a tendency to drop out of those institutions in which structures for the reintegration of the teaching acts are not satisfactorily achieved.
2. Distance students have difficulty achieving quality of learning in those institutions in which structures for the reintegration of the teaching acts are not satisfactorily achieved.
3. The status of learning at a distance may be questioned in those institutions in which the reintegration of the teaching acts is not satisfactorily achieved.

Simonson, Smaldino, Albright and Zvacek (2009) conclude their recent book chapter on Theories of Distance Education with the following:

> The changing and diverse environment in which distance education is practiced has inhibited the development of a single theory upon which to base practice and research. A variety of theories have been proposed to describe traditional distance education. These

theories emphasize that distance education is a fundamentally different form of education. Recent emerging theories, based on the capabilities of new interactive audio and video systems, state that distance education is not a distinct field of education. Both utilization of existing educational theory and the creation of like experiences for both the distant and local learner emphasized. Traditional distance education theorists will need to address the changes to distance education facilitated by new technologies.... An environment in which technology, society, economics, politics and theories of learning are all in transition suggests that definition, theories and practice of distance education will continue to be contested.

3

Models of Distance Education

A number of attempts have been made to integrate the defining features of distance education into models of distance education. Rumble (1986) presents three such models.

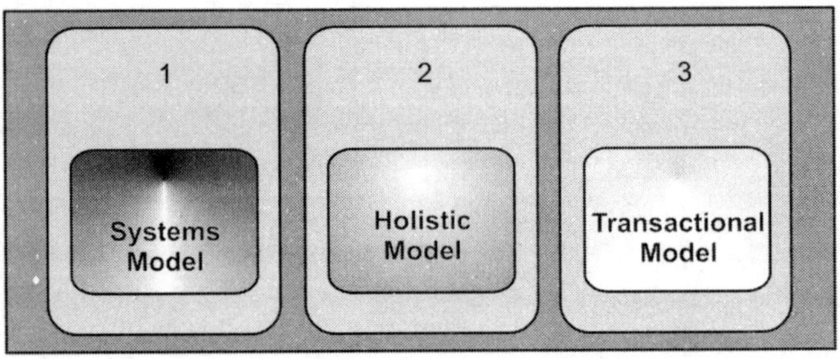

The Systems Model of Distance Education

Kaye and Rumble (1978) proposed the systems Model of Distance Education. They based this model on the concepts developed by Miller and Rice for analyzing organizations as open systems. Miller and Rice (1967) categorized the activities carried out by an organization into three: (a) operating activities, (b) logistical activities and (c) regulatory activities. The operating activities characterizing distance education can be grouped into two major subsystems: (a) the material subsystem and (b) the student subsystem. The significance of this model is that it clearly identifies the main activities involved in operating a distance education enterprise, as well as the inter-relationships between them. It focuses the importance of the quasi-industrial processes that characterizes the production and distribution of materials and emphasizes the specialization of tasks and division of labour.

The Holistic Model of Distance Education

This model is developed by Perraton (2000). It is a linked sequence of fourteen elements of distance education provision. Rumble explains the logic of the model in the following way:

> Educational media are similar in their effectiveness, but differ in the ways they can readily be distributed. This makes it possible to move away from the fixed staffing ratios necessary to ensure face-to-face study, thereby changing the role of the teacher and making possible a reduction in costs. It is then possible to reach audiences different from the traditional ones, through distance teaching, and to do so at a reasonable cost. The equivalence of the media however, presents us with problems of choice, best resolved by a multi-media approach which allows for feedback and encourages active learning. In working out the approach to be used, the organization of any face-to-face element is of key importance and leads us to consider how to use distance teaching to ensure dialogue – something which is facilitated if a concern with new audiences and a new relation between education and the community lead to the use of groups as a basis for adult learning.

The Transactional Model of Distance Education

This model views distance education from the competing perspectives of the main actors in the process and the relationships or transactions between them. In distance education, learners have three main types of transaction

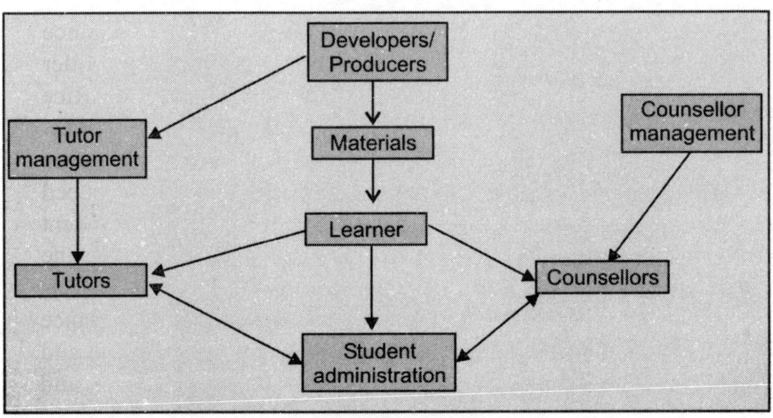

A Transactional Model

to maintain, and each of these has a different state within the system: (a) transactions with the learning materials, (b) transactions with intermediaries such as tutors, counselors etc, and (c) transactions with the institution. Viewing distance education systems in transactional terms emphasizes the human relations aspects of management, in contrast to the systems approach.

Moore and Kearsley (2005) presented a general model that describes the main component processes and elements of a distance education system.

There must be:

- a source of knowledge that is to be taught and learned
- a subsystem to structure them into materials and activities for students (courses)
- another subsystem that delivers the courses to learners
- teachers who interact with learners as they use these materials in making their knowledge
- learners in their different environments
- a subsystem that monitors and evaluates outcomes so that interventions are possible where failures occur.
- an organizations with a policy and a management structure to link these different prices.

A General Model for Distance Education by Moore and Kearsley

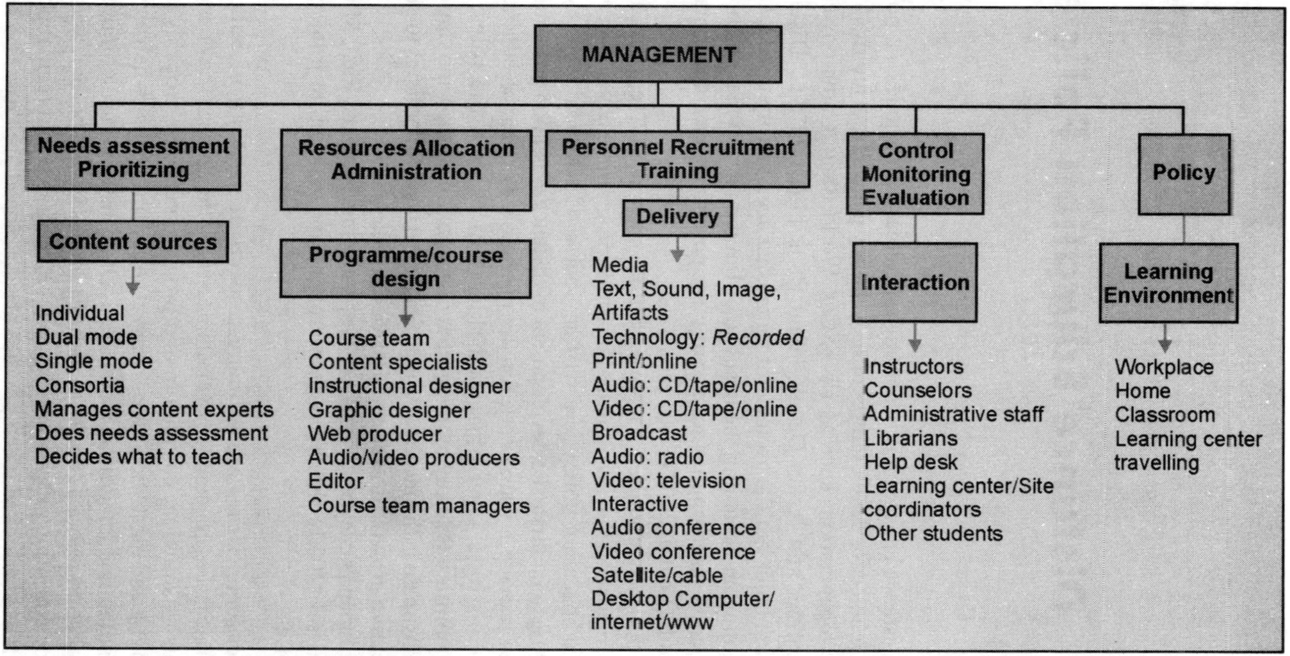

The elements indicated above are the content, design, communications technologies, interaction, learning environment and management that are essential subsystems in every distance education organization.

4

Distance Education Policies

Distance education is becoming an increasingly significant policy choice for developing countries. Policy papers from international organizations such as UNESCO, World Bank, Commonwealth of Learning, and Asian Development Bank highlight this. Distance education holds out the promise of increasing accessibility to education and training and enabling the best use of limited educational resources. But, what is surprising is the lack of clear policy for open and distance education (Lental, 2004).

A policy is a written course of action, such as statute, procedure, rule or regulation that is adopted to facilitate programme development. A distance education policy is a written course of action adopted by an institution to facilitate the development of distance education programme. Policies provide a framework for the operation of distance education. They constitute a set of agreed rules that explain the roles and responsibilities. One key indicator that distance education is moving into the mainstream is the increased emphasis or the need for policies to guide its effective growth Simson and Bauck (2003).

Gellman Danley and Fetzner (1998) and King, Naugent, Eich, Mlinek and Russel (2000) divided policies for distance education into seven categories.

Academic issues are in many respects at the heart of policies. Academic issues concern the overall integrity of the course. They concern students' instruction, curriculum and programme. They probably have the longest and most wide spread impact. Academic policies help ensure that institutional integrity is maintained. Once institutional commitment to distance education is made, academic policies should be reviewed and distance education programmes should be integrated into regulations.

Often overlooked when policies are developed are those that relate

Policies of Distance Education

I Academic Policies	
A. Students	1. Admission policies 2. Grading policies 3. Academic records
B. Faculty	1. Evaluation 2. Credentials
C. Curriculum	1. Accreditation 2. Course/programme approval 3. course/programme evaluation
II Fiscal, Geographic, and Governance Policies	
A. Fiscal	1. Tuition collection and disbursement 2. Special fees 3. State funding 4. Administrative costs 5. Telecommunications costs
B. Geographic	1. In-district vs. out-of-district 2. Consortia agreements
C. Governance	1. Board oversight 2. Consortia contracts 3. Provider constracts
III Faculty Policies	
A. Compensation	1. Design and development incentives 2. Overload compensation
B. Evaluation	1. Course evaluation 2. Promotion and contract 3. Intellectual freedom
C. Support	1. Staff development/training 2. Course/programme support 3. Local facilitators
IV Legal Policies	
A. Intellectual property	
B. Copyright	
C. Liability	1. Student 2. Faculty 3. School
V Student Policies	
A. Academic	1. Advising 2. Resources and laboratories 3. Training 4. Testing and assessment
B. Nonacademic	1. Equipment and software 2. Financial aid 3. Privacy 4. Access and equity
VI Technical Policies	
A. System	
B. Contractual agreements	
VII Philosophical Policies	
A. Vision	
B. Mission	
C. Activities	

to the vision, mission and understanding distance education. When an educational organization decides to become involved in offering distance education its vision and mission statements should respect its commitment to distance education.

From a policy perspective, the factors that national educational policy makers have to consider were identified by Dodds and Youngman (2004) some years ago. They are:

- The rational for the development of distance education and its priority in relation to other options.
- The perceived needs for distance education and the appropriate levels of provision, namely secondary, tertiary, and adult basic education.
- The direct costs and opportunity costs of investing in distance education provision and the potential cost-benefits.
- The appropriate institutional arrangements and the capacity for developing and maintaining an effective distance-education system in terms of the recurrent resources, management capability, trained staff, materials production, student support and (information) communications infrastructure.
- The status of distance education and the acceptability of its qualifications within the national system of educational credentials.
- The possibilities for international cooperation in developing and sustaining a distance-education system.

Jegede and Okebukola (2002) note from their experience of Nigeria, nations wanting to develop distance education are in hurry and need road-maps to guide them. What might a road-map look like? What are the signposts on the road? What are the critical issues in policy and planning for distance education systems?

They are:

- Identifying the target population and their needs.
- Choosing the type of system,
- Choosing the appropriate technology of delivering,
- Business planning and costing distance education systems.
- Materials-developing or acquiring.
- Tutoring and supporting students.
- Recruiting and enrolling students,
- Assessing students,

- Managing and administering the distance education system.
- Monitoring, evaluation and quality assurance.

This list indicates the areas of decision-making and highlights the range of decisions policy makers and planners have to address in establishing and maintaining distance education systems.

5

Classification of Distance Education Institutions

Distance education institutions are of various types. It is difficult to scientifically classify them because of diversity in them. Institutions range from primary schools to universities. They have different structures, goals, funding, etc. They defy any systematic categorization. It is somewhat easy to classify distance higher education institutions. Hence, focus here is on higher level distance institutions.

Classification of Distance Teaching Institutions by Otto Peters, El-Bushra, Neil, Keegan and Rumble

Otto Peters (1971) presented a two-fold classification of institutions of distance teaching at university level by grouping institutions into Western models and Eastern models. It was the first systematic classification. This classification is based on the differences in administration and didactic structures between a study programme based on printed materials plus correspondence or media communication in Western models and printed materials plus face to face contacts in Eastern models.

Peter's classification has four bases: a) Political structure, b) Organizational structure, c) Curriculum structure and d) Didactic structure. The Eastern models in Peter's typology were given up in the early 1990s, though some aspects of the models survive in China.

El-Bushra (1973) identified six categories of correspondence teaching at university level:

- Institutions dealing exclusively with external students (e.g. the UKOU).
- Institutions which offer facilities for external examinations but provide no actual teaching (e.g. the External Degrees Service of the University of London).

- Institutions where the correspondence unit operates under a single department (e.g., The School of Education at the University of South Pacific).
- Institutions which accept both internal and external students in the same teaching department and in which the correspondence unit is an administrative and supervisory body (e.g. the University of New England in Australia).
- Institutions where the correspondence department takes responsibility not only for administering the courses, but also for teaching them (e.g. the University of Queensland in Australia).
- Institutions which offer correspondence courses in co-operation with other bodies (e.g. Massey University in New Zealand).

Neil (1981) distinguished between autonomous distance learning systems and those which operate as distance learning wings of conventional institutions. He saw institutional autonomy from four areas of control - finance, examination and accreditation, curriculum and materials, and delivery and student support system. On the basis of institutional autonomy, Neil identified five types of distance learning systems:

- Centre-periphery model.
- Associated centre model.
- Dispersed centre model.
- Switchboard organization model.
- Service institution model.

Keegan and Rumble (1982) identified seven types of universities which teach at a distance on the basis of the autonomy of the institutions:

- Autonomous, centrally controlled distance teaching universities (OU UK, EU, UNED)
- Autonomous, decentralized distance teaching universities (UNED Spain)
- Essentially autonomous distance teaching universities operating within a federated university structure (TU Quebec)
- Autonomous centralized distance teaching system with a high degree of control using facilities based in and run by conventional universities (DDR)
- Mixed mode, uni-departmental model (External Studies Department, University of Queensland)

- Mixed mode, multi-departmental model (New England model)
- Mixed mode, multi institutional model (Massey University, New Zealand)

Keegan (1986) classified distance teaching institutions into two broad types: autonomous institutions and mixed institutions. Autonomous institutions are again divided into two groups, while mixed institutions are divided into three groups. Fundamental to this classification is the acceptance of the basic difference between autonomous distance teaching institutions and distance subsections of conventional institutions. This classification is based on six premises for the construction of a useful typology:

- It should be helpful to readers to enable them to distinguish one type from other.
- It should be helpful to have each group containing a large number of institutions.
- It should not be artificial with regard to students. Each group must enroll a large number of students.
- It should not be artificial with regard to time. Each group must have been in existence for at least a decade, preferably longer.
- It should try to encompass all distance teaching institutions, public or private, at all levels from primary to postgraduate levels.
- It should include those distance teaching institutions or departments of existing institutions which exhibit both the major characteristic subsystems of distance institutions.

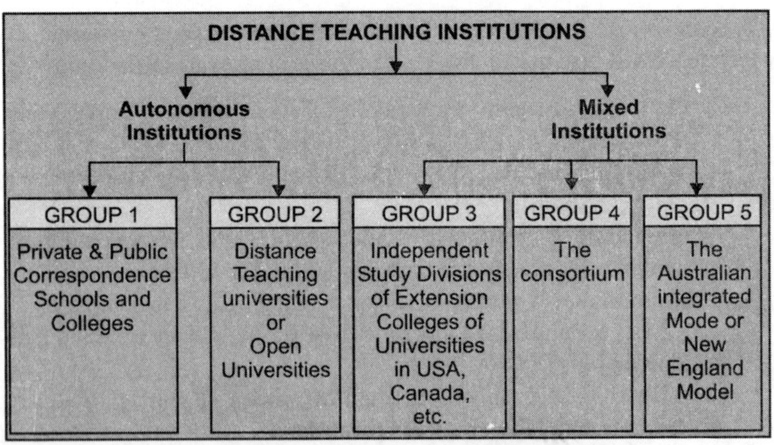

Keegan's Typology of Distance Teaching Institutions

John Daniel, the former Vice-Chancellor of the British Open University, distinguished between four dominant higher distance education institutions: (a) the mega universities, (b) the other distance teaching universities, (c) the dual mode institutions, and (d) the ad hoc technology based teaching systems.

A.W. Bates (2005) attempted to summarize the increasing diversification of distance education provision on a global base.

Types of Distance Education Institutions

1. Public distance education institutions
   - National Open Universities
   - Public Online Universities
   - Virtual Institutions
2. Dual Mode institutions
3. For-profit distance education institutions
   - Private Universities
   - University for a Profits
4. Partnerships and Consortia
   - University and college point degrees
   - Public-private partnership
   - State/national consortia
   - For profit consortia
5. Workshop training
6. Virtual schools

Advantages of Autonomous Distance Teaching Universities (DTUs)

Rumble and Harry believed that:

- Autonomous DTUs are generally more advantageous for (1) external students, in that they are wholly dedicated to their needs, and (2) the nation, in that they can more readily respond to national needs which can only be met by distance means.
- Autonomous DTUs more readily cater for the needs of distant students to the extent that there are marked differences between them and students in conventional systems.
- Autonomous DTUs are administratively more efficient given the requisite volume of students.
- There is less likelihood of competition between DTUs because, by their very nature, they are costly to establish and hence there is unlikely to be more than one of them in all but the very largest

countries. This conclusion lies in with Otto Peters' forecast in the late 1960s that, if DTUs were founded, they would be industrialized organizations with monopolistic tendencies.

- The costs associated with the establishment of an infrastructure for a DTU and the preparation of sufficient course materials to support a degree programme are high, and require a guaranteed annual volume of student enrolments if the system is to be cost-efficient. If sufficient numbers of students cannot be guaranteed, a mixed system is preferable.
- The number of students at which an autonomous DTU becomes more efficient than a mixed-mode institution depends on the choice of media, the extent of the students support services, and the number of courses on offer, as well as the costs of conventional university education in the country concerned.

Rumble and Harry (1982) while comparing the strengths and weaknesses of Distance Teaching Universities (DTUs) and Campus Based Universities (CBUs) indicated the following strengths of autonomous Distance Teaching Universities (DTUs):

- Distance education may be best carried out in institutions dedicated to it.
- Administrative structures of CBUs are not suited to the development and management of distance education.
- The needs of part-time adult distance students will be better served in an institution that is wholly dedicated to their needs.
- DTUs once established develop important strengths in the technology and processes of material development and the delivery of support services to distant students.
- DTUs are capable of achieving greater economies of scale.

6

Distance Teaching Universities

Distance teaching universities (DTUs) are the dominant structural forms of distance higher education. Distance teaching universities created a revolution by making higher education more accessible and less costly. DTUs are called by different names such as 'Universities Without Walls', 'Tele Universities', 'Universities of Air', 'Correspondence Universities', 'Open Universities'.

Since the establishment of the UKOU, a good number of Open Universities came into existence in both the developed and developing countries. Names of some of well-established open universities in the world are given on the next page.

The concept of 'open university' has revolutionized contemporary educational thinking. As an institution, open university is regarded as a powerful instrument for equalizing higher educational 'opportunities and leveling educational imbalances. Open university has become a valued component of many national educational policies, programmes and practices. It is a great educational innovation of modern times. It is called by different names. Of late, the terms 'Virtual University' and 'Online University' are also used. The most popular name is 'open university'. This term entered the English language with the creation of the Open University in the UK in 1969, although that institution was originally called the University of Air when the idea was floated. Its planners thought that the name of the University should reflect the goal it was to pursue (opening access to higher education).

The foundation of the Open University in the United Kingdom (UKOU) in 1969 marked the beginning of a new and prestigious era in the history of distance higher education. Although Centre National d'Enseignement a 'Distance (France) and University of South Africa (South Africa) have longer institutional histories, most observers consider

Open Universities in the World

S. No.	Name	Country	Year of Establishment
1.	University of South Africa	RSA	1946
2.	Open University	UK	1969
3.	Allama Iqbal University	Pakistan	1975
4.	Athabasca University	Canada	1975
5.	Open University	Israel	1974
6.	Fern Universitat	Germany	1974
7.	Payame Noor University	Iran	1987
8.	Sri Lanka Open University	Sri Lanka	1980
9.	Sukhothai Thammathirat Open University	Thailand	1978
10.	Central Radio and Television University	China	1979
11.	University of Air	Japan	1983
12.	Korea National University	Korea	1982
13.	Korea Air and Correspondence University	South Korea	1981
14.	Open Universiteit	Netherlands	1981
15.	Universitas Terbuka	Indonesia	1984
16.	Universidad Nacional De Education a distancia	Spain	1972
17.	Universidad Nacional Abierta	Venezuela	1977
18.	Universidad Estatal a Distancia	Costa Rica	1977
19.	Open University	Tanzania	1992
20.	Al-Quds Open University	Jordan	1986
21.	Universidade Aberta	Portugal	1988
22.	National Open University	Taiwan	1986
23.	Open University	Hong Kong	1989
24.	The Open University of Hochiminh	Vietnam	1990
25.	Anadolu University	Turkey	1982
26.	Bangladesh Open University	Bangladesh	1995
33.	Al-Quda Open University	Palestine	1991
38.	Zimbabwe Open University	Zimbabwe	1999

the UKOU as the pioneer of modern distance education at university level. Because of this reason, its programmes and activities attracted considerable interest throughout the world. The first Vice-Chancellor of the UKOU vividly described its creation and early development (Perry, 1976). He narrated how the grand concept came into being, how apparently unyielding new ground was broken … above all how Britain led the World into a historic new educational dimension (Wilson, 1976). Till 1969 educational authorities in several countries were sceptical in

Open Universities in India

S. No.	Open University	City/Town	State	Year of Estd.
1.	Indira Gandhi National Open University (IGNOU)	New Delhi	New Delhi	1985
2.	Dr. B.R. Ambedkar Open University (BRAOU)	Hyderabad	Andhra Pradesh	1982
3.	Nalanda Open University (NOU)	Patna	Bhiar	1987
4.	Vardhaman Mahveer Open University (VMOU)	Kota	Rajasthan	1987
5.	Y.C. Maharashtra Open University (YCMOU)	Nashik	Maharashtra	1989
6.	M.P. Bhoj Open University (MPBOU)	Bhopal	Madhya Pradesh	1992
7.	Dr. Babasahod Ambedkar Open Univerisity (BAOU)	Ahmedbad	Gujarat	1994
8.	Karnataka State Open University (KOU)	Mysore	Karnataka	1996
9.	Netaji Subash Open University (NSOU)	Calcutta	West Bengal	1997
10.	Rajarshi Tandon UP Open University (RTUPOU)	Allahabad	Uttar Pradesh	1999
11.	Tamil Nadu Open University (TNOU)	Madras	Tamil Nadu	2002
12.	Pt. Sunderlal Sharma (Open) University (PSLOU)	Bilaspur	Chattishgrah	2005
13.	Uttaranchal Open University (UOU)	Haldwani	Uttaranchal	2005
14.	Krishna Kant Handique State Open University	Guwahati	Assam	2005
15.	Global Open University	Kohima	Nagaland	2006

their estimate of distance education institutions. The establishment of a totally public funded and autonomous University adopting distance teaching methods changed the situation. In the 1970s and in the following years, a good number of open universities came into being in both the developed and developing countries.

History

The idea of open university occurred to some individuals and institutions even before the establishment of the UKOU. Stuart Marriot (Marriot, 1981) discovered in an article published in *The University Extension Journal* in 1891:

> "Before long some university will seize the unequalled opportunity … will broadly lay down a curriculum of study for degrees in new lines suited to the needs of those who desire to carry on their intellectual culture side by side with the regular business of life."

In an American radio magazine in 1922 appeared the words (Tunstall, 1974):

> "The people's University of the Air will have a greater student body than all over universities put together."

In 1926 in England, J.C. Stobart, author of two reliable pieces of higher popular education, *The Glory that was Greece* and *The Grandeur that was Rome*, mooted something similar (Tunstall, 1974).

Historically, the University of South Africa is the first open university. The University of South Africa began as the University of the Cape of Good Hope in 1873 as an examining body for affiliated university colleges. In 1916 it was established as a Federation of Colleges. By the end of Second World War the colleges became autonomous and independent and the University slowly and gradually concentrated on external studies. In 1946 The University of South Africa became a teaching as well as an examining institution. This is the first public university in the World to teach exclusively by means of distance education (DETC NEWS, 2002).

In 1962 Michael Young proposed an open university to prepare people for external degrees of London University. But his energies went into the establishment of National Extension College.

Establishment of UK Open University

In 1963 two events occurred of some importance to the emergence of the UKOU. One was the publication of the Robbins Report on Higher Education, the Report of the Committee appointed in 1961 under the chairmanship of Lord Robbins to review the pattern of full time higher education in Great Britain. The Robbins Committee did not make any firm suggestion for an institution like the open university, but it mentioned the potential value of 'the establishment by some universities of correspondence courses'. The second event of 1963 was the succession of Harold Wilson to the leadership of the Labour Party. Harold Wilson, before he became the leader of the Labour Party, was greatly impressed by the higher education in the USA. He saw the immense potential of television in every home. Harold Wilson also knew well the Soviet use of radio and correspondence courses for degree teaching. The influence of

United States and Soviet Russia influenced Harold Wilson to conceive a vision in which television and radio would be used to bring higher education into every home in the UK. Harold Wilson outlined his scheme for a University of the Air in an election campaign speech in Glasgow in 1963. He envisaged this as a consortium of existing universities using broadcasting and correspondence tuition to bring their teaching to adult students in their homes. When Labour Party came to power, Wilson handed over the responsibility for realising his dream to Jennie Lee, who was at the time Under Secretary of State for Education and Science. As the ideas developed, Jennie Lee made it clear that she wanted an autonomous, independent, university equal to any other. She overcame the scepticism and even hostility of the educational establishment by 'outsnobbing the snobs', as she put it herself. She brought together a Planning Committee which included five Vice-Chancellors, the Principal of a Polytechnic, and the leaders of two education authorities. Their recommendations won the support of Jennie Lee's colleagues in the Cabinet, and the Open University at last became government policy, and shortly afterwards, a reality.

Perry (1976) the founder Vice-Chancellor of the UKOU, recalling the initial years of the University noted:

> Academics all over Britain accept that the Open University has succeeded, that distance learning works and that the Open University graduates are as good as any others. They (these graduates) have been accepted by every other British University in postgraduate courses without any question.
> The quality of the courses is seen and is commended by the academic world. The quality of the students, the quality of the exams—they are all recognized by the academics in other universities. But emotionally, many of them don't accept it all. Emotionally there still is a strong feeling that on-campus teaching in the face-to-face situation is the one way of actually teaching and that this is the vital thing in order to train scholars for the future. It may take decades rather than years to overcome this emotional reaction. You have to remember, I suppose, that every advance in education has been resisted for years and years. When we tried to introduce universal primary education, people argued that losing child labour out of coal mines would cause economic unrest. The same sort of people objected to universal secondary education because it was going to over educate the working classes

who ought to be kept in their place and learn a trade. I suppose the same reaction occurs to the idea of universal tertiary education or certainly the opportunity for it.

Peters (2008) felt that open universities are modern and reflective of contemporary societal needs. He noted:

> It is significant to see that the open universities represent a new type of university that is in accordance with marked political and educational trends: the democratization of university study, mass higher education, lifelong education, adult higher education, professional qualifications, collaboration with the labour market and globalization.

Writing about ten autonomous multimedia distance teaching universities, Rumble and Harry (1982) agreed that these universities employed:

- a conscious and systematic approach to the design of learning materials for independent study,
- the use of a wide range of media and other resources to teach,
- the centralized design and production of materials to combined localized learning,
- the provision of two-way communication between students and tutors who generally operate at a distance from the student but with the possibility of occasional meetings,
- the introduction of a number of quasi-industrial process, and
- extensive and well defined administrative areas

Why Distance Teaching Universities?

The reasons for setting up distance teaching universities, according to Borje Holmberg (1986), are mainly:

- the need felt in many countries to increase the offer of university education generally,
- a realization that adults, with jobs, family and social commitments constituted a large group of prospective part-university students,
- a wish to serve both individuals and society by offering study opportunities to adults, among them disadvantaged groups,
- the need found in many professions for further training at an advanced level,

- a wish to support educational innovation,
- a belief in the feasibility of an economical use of educational resources by mediated teaching.

These reasons find expression in the aims and objectives of almost all distance teaching universities. The important aims and objectives of some major distance teaching/open universities are given in the following paragraphs.

Aims and Objectives of Some Distance Teaching Universities

Indira Gandhi National Open University (India)

- to advance and disseminate learning and knowledge by a diversity of means including the use of communication technology
- to provide opportunities for higher education to a large segment of the population
- to promote the educational well being of the community
- to encourage the open university and distance education system in the educational pattern of the country.

Universities Terbuka (Indonesia)

- to provide more opportunities for access to higher education, using distance means
- to provide high level manpower for various sectors of development
- to upgrade people working in education and in various professional jobs

Korea Air and Correspondence University (Korea)

- to raise the general educational level of the people by providing opportunities of higher education to those high school graduates who, for various reasons, cannot pursue ordinary college education.
- to improve the academic and professional qualifies of people engaged in the professional fields covered by the twelve major areas of study in order to contribute to the national welfare through higher education.

Allama Iqbal Open University (Pakistan)

- to provide facilities to people who cannot leave their homes and jobs in such a manner as it may determine.

- to provide such facilities to the masses for their education uplift as it may determine.
- to provide facilities for the training of teachers in such a manner as it may determine.
- to provide for instruction in such branches of learning technology or vocation as it may deem fit, and to make provision for research and for the advancement and dissemination of knowledge in such manner as it may determine.
- to hold examinations, to award and confer degrees, diplomas, and other academic distinctions.

Sukhothoi Thammathirat Open University (Thailand)

- to provide and promote university and professional education so as to enable the people to raise their educational standards in response to the needs of society.
- to promote research so as to generate new knowledge and to national development.
- to render public services to society by disseminating knowledge so as to promote personal development and professional competence.
- to preserve and develop national culture.

The University of the Air (Japan)

- to provide working people and housewives with the change of life long university level education.
- to provide an innovative and flexible system of university level education which is open to all high school graduates
- to cooperate with existing universities and make full use the latest knowledge and nearest educational technology in order to offer a system of higher education which meets contemporary needs.

Universidad National de Education a Distancia (Spain)

- to provide higher education at home, equivalent to that provided by the conventional universities to all those who have missed their first educational opportunity or were unable to attend existing institutions of learning.
- to substitute the free learning offered in the traditional universities to those who could not attend teachers and hence had to study independently.

- to create an effective instrument to achieve equal opportunities in higher education.
- to develop a more individualised and student centered system of teaching and learning.
- to contribute to the methodological innovation in the Spanish higher education system.

Universidad Nacional Abierta (Venezuela)

- to offer real educational opportunities at the higher education level to students from different socio-economic classes in the society and especially to adults and those members of the working population who have not previously had the opportunity to attend a traditional institutions.
- to meet in part the social demand for higher education at a standard not inferior to those of the best higher educational institutions in the country
- to contribute to the autonomous development of the country by meeting its needs for trained human resources, in scientific and technological fields.
- to establish institution structures and processes capable of continuous development and of incorporating innovations that will optimise the teaching-learning process.
- to develop a teaching-learning system relevant to the conditions, needs and aspirations of its students, and conducive to the stimulation of the students' capacity for creativity and critical thinking.
- to support the development needs of the nation in collaboration with other relevant agencies and institutions.
- to contribute to a significant diminution of unit costs in higher education.
- to provide its educational programmes throughout the country.
- to optimise the productive use of free time by persons following its programmes.

From the charters of various distance teaching universities/open universities the following broad objectives can be identified;

- to expand opportunities for higher education
- to provide higher education to those who cannot leave their homes and jobs
- to improve academic and professional qualifications of people engaged in professions

- to raise general well educational level of society
- to provide training for teachers
- to obtain reduction in education costs.
- to develop a more individualised and student centred system of teaching and learning
- to support reforms in education, and
- to democratise and revolutionise education

Openness of Open Universities

The term, 'open', has many meanings, and the aura of most of them seem generous and 'charismatic' – open-handed, open-ended, open-hearted, open house, open choice. 'Open' as contrasted with 'closed' carries suggestions of the lessening or removal of restrictions, of exclusions and of privilege; of demolishing or lowering established barriers between subject areas; of enlarging and enriching the areas of activity and experience graded as educational.

Perhaps the most commonly used sense of 'open' has been the idea of creating opportunities for study for those debarred from it for whatever reasons, be it lack of formal education attainments or shortage of vacancies, poverty, remoteness, employment or domestic necessities. To seek increased access is, of course, not a recent objective amongst educators. It has a long, honourable history of pioneer efforts, over a hundred years or more. London University was created in 1836 as a body to conduct examinations and award degrees and by 1858 admitted matriculation candidates from any part of the world. The work in the United Kingdom of such voluntary agencies as the Workers' Educational Association, the Extension Services and the extramural departments of universities is another expression of the same intention. It has parallels in many other countries, perhaps most notably in the Soviet Union, where nearly half the students in higher education study are on a part-time basis. Openness in that sense is no new phenomenon.

This 'openness' is the cardinal feature of the distance teaching universities. It is often said that the British Open University's "uniqueness lies not merely in its application of modern communication technology, but also in its philosophical concept of openness".

In what sense are open universities "open"? The following four characteristics are the ones most frequently citied:

- Openness with regard to person, regardless of prior academic qualifications and without any entrance examination. Essentially it is the students, not the institute who controls the decision of enrolments.

- Openness with regard to place (and sometimes pace) of study. While there may be voluntary study centres or even residential summer schools, there is not central campus or specific time and place of study; every home can be a campus.
- Openness with regard to studies, generally there are few required subjects and emphasis is placed on broad studies, independent choice of courses and application of efforts. Guided self-learning, not teaching, is the principal mode of instruction.
- Openness with regard to completion, deferment, temporary discontinuation or termination of studies.

The 'open' of a open university (Dutch Open University) is well explained by Pierre Morin the following way:

- 'open' means that the Open University does not impose any formal admission requirements and does not demand any formal proof of preliminary knowledge, nor is there an entrance examination. Both before and during the learning process the students have to decide for themselves whether they are capable of studying successfully.
- 'open' also means that the students are allowed a great deal of freedom in planning their courses of study. Strictly speaking there are no fixed degree programmes as such. First, a student can study one or two courses separately. A course usually contains one or two modules, representing one or two hundred hours of study. Secondly, when the students have followed several courses and have passed the exams, they can ask for a statement or dossier (dossioma, portfolio) of all the courses they have completed. Thirdly, Open University can recognize a series of courses by conferring an Open University degree. Finally, the Open University has designed a number of combinations of courses in such a way that they lead to degrees which are equal or almost equal to certain degrees in higher vocational or university education. However, students remain free to choose their own path through that combination.
- A third form of openness is the students' freedom to choose their own pace of study. In principle, the students can start a course whenever they want, and the Open University holds several examinations in each subject every year. Naturally, every

course requires an element of pacing, which also goes for the supervision.

- However, the students remain completely free to use those facilities in whichever way they choose. This means that openness in the fourth place allows the Open University to leave the students alone with the learning material, although they can always ask for advice and supervision at the study centres. The students themselves really decide where and how they study.

British Open University's Openness

The first Chancellor of the British Open University, the late Lord Crowther, in his address, after receiving The Royal Charter in 1969, said that the Open University would be open, not only as to entry, but as to place, as to method and as to ideas. His address is worth reproducing here:

- We are open, first, as to people. Not for us the carefully regulated escalation from one educational level to the next by which the traditional universities establish their criteria for admission. The first, and most urgent, task before us is to cater for the many thousands of people, fully capable of a higher education, who, for one reason or another, do not get it, or do not get as much of it as they can turn to advantage or as they discover, sometimes too late, that they need. Only in recent years have we come to realize how many such people there are, and how large are the gaps in educational provision through which they can fall. The existing system, for all its expansion, misses and leaves aside a great unused reservoir of human talent and potential. Men and women drop out through failures in the system, through disadvantages of their environment, through mistakes of their own judgment, through sheer bad luck. These are our primary material. To them we offer a further opportunity.

  But if this were all, we could hardly call ourselves a University. This is not simply an educational rescue mission - though that is our first task, and we do not decry it. But we also aim wider and higher. Wherever there is an unprovoked need for higher education, supplementing the existing provision, there is our constituency….

  The Open University is not the rival of the existing universities. It is designed to take over where they are compelled to leave off…..

- We are open as to places. This University has no cloisters – a word meaning closed. Hardly even shall we have a campus. By a very happy chance, our only local habitation will be in the new city that is to bear two of the widest-ranging names in the history of English thought, Milton Keynes. But this is only where the tip of our toe touches ground. The rest of the University will be disembodied and airborne. From the start, it will flow all over the United Kingdom.....
- We are open as to methods. We start, in dependence on, in grateful partnership with, the BBC. But already the development of technology is marching on, and I predict that before long actual broadcasting will form only a small part of the University's output. The world is caught in a Communications Revolution.... Every new form of human communication will be examined to see how it can be used to raise and broaden the level of human understanding....
- We are open, finally, to ideas. It has been said that there are two aspects of education, both necessary. One regards the individual human mind as a vessel of varying capacity, into which is to be poured as much as it will hold of the knowledge and experience by which human society lives and moves. This is the Martha of education - and we shall have plenty of these tasks to perform. But the Mary regards the human mind more as a fire that has to be set alight and blown with the divine afflatus. That also we take as our ambition.....

Mega Universities

Open universities have created a revolution by making higher education more accessible and less costly. This is especially true of the mega-universities, which are defined by John Daniel (1996), the Former Vice-Chancellor of the UKOU as distance teaching universities with over 1,00,000 students in degree programmes.

There were ten such institutions when Jon Daniel first published his book *Mega Universities and Knowledge Media: Technology Strategies for Higher Education* in 1996.

In 1999 there were 11 such institutions enrolling about 3 million students between them and they are listed here.

Today the number of mega universities doubled and student enrollments have tripled and new mega universities are on the horizon. The 1,00,000 enrolment criterion is an arbitrary cut-off classification.

Mega Universities: Enrollment and Unit Cost

Name of the Institution	*Country*	*Enrollment*	*Unit Cost*
China TV University System	China	530,000	40
Centre National d'Enseignement a Distance	France	184,614	50
Indira Gandhi National Open University	India	242,000	35
Universitas Terbuka	Indonesia	353,000	15
Payame Noor University	Iran	117,000	25
Korea National Open University	Korea	210,578	05
University of South Africa	South-Arica	133,000	50
Universidad National de Education a Distance	Spain	110,000	40
Sukhothai Thammathirat Open University	Thailand	216,800	30
Anadolu University	Turkey	577,804	10
The Open University	UK	157,450	50

The mega university experience, as a particular form of distance education practice, has gained a rich and extensive experience in both the highly industrialized and the developing regions of our world.

In many respects, the practice of distance education in the mega universities context is unique when compared to other forms of distance education and face-to-face higher education provision. Further, the mega university, as institution, has the most extensive experience in technology mediated learning. It is unique innovation in the higher education sphere with global relevance. In the words of John Daniel and Wayne Mackintosh (2003) "the mega university system, as one of the most important innovations in higher education of the 20th century has successfully combined the challenges of access and quality in an approach that can be scaled up in ways that reduce cost without compromising the core social values of the university.

These institutions have greatly increased access to higher education in their countries while at the same time lowering the costs of university education in dramatic fashion. Most of the mega-open universities teach each student for less than half of the average cost per student in the other universities of their countries. Furthermore, in most of the mega universities student fees provide more than half of the budget of the institution. At a time when governments are finding it increasingly difficult to respond to all the financial demands made upon them, the success of the mega-universities in reducing the cost of higher education has important implications for public policy. The mega-universities share some common characteristics such as:

- Role in national policy
- Access to communication facilities
- Linkages to the rest of higher education
- Students
- Curriculum
- Cost-effectiveness
- Operational systems
- Quality and recognition
- International role

Mega Universities of the World

Name of the Institution	*Country*	*Founded*	*Abbreviation*
China TV University System	China	1979	CTVU
Center National d'Enseignement a Distance	France	1939	CNED
Indira Gandhi National Open University	India	1985	IGNOU
Universitas Terbuka	Indonesia	1984	UT
Payame Noor University	Iran	1987	PNU
Korea National Open University	Korea	1982	KNOU
University of South Africa	South Africa	1873	UNISA
Universidad Nacional de Educacion a Distance	Spain	1972	UNED
Sukhothai Thammathirat Open University	Thailand	1978	STOU
Anadolu University	Turkey	1982	AU
The Open University	UK	1969	UKOU

7

Organizational Structure of Distance Education Systems

Distance education systems with similar goals can be organized in different ways, reflecting philosophical, social, cultural, political, geographical, historical and technological differences. There is therefore no single right way of organizing a distance education system. But all structures are to consider the functions of a system.

Distance educators and researchers made attempts to identify the functions carried out by distance education systems. Rumble (1986) identified the following functions undertaken by a distance teaching system:

- Curriculum planning.
- Materials development - production, storage and delivery.
- Students' recruitment - admission and counseling.
- Organization of study facilities and support services.
- Tutoring, assessment and examinations of students.
- Monitoring of students progress.
- General and specialist administration and management.
- Research and evaluation.

The range of media used in distance teaching systems provides an added dimension to the tasks which need to be undertaken.

The research findings on organizational design point towards a continuous process of evolution of the structure as the scope of activities of the institution expands in terms of its concept as well as geographical coverage. Therefore, there is no one optimal structure design which would always serve a strategy with maximum efficiency and effectiveness. However, it would be advisable for an institutional planner, according to Ram Reddy (1987), to keep the following factors in mind while deciding about the institutional structure:

- It must encourage innovation on the part of academics, staff, students and all the other associates.
- It must service the institutional objectives both in the short and long run.
- It must facilitate the institutional communication process both within and outside with various interest groups.
- It must contribute towards organizational climate by encouraging participation rather than isolation, between the various officials and academics, and between the institution and the outside world.
- It should facilitate decision making and various implementation processes.
- It must fulfill the aspiration for professional growth of officials and academics, and
- It must provide for task role clarity for various agencies and top officials involved in the implementation. The stability of top-level leadership is also an essential requirement of the structuring process.

Rumble (1986) mentions three ways in which organizations carrying out the basic functions of distance teaching system can be structured:

1. Classic organization model. It is a purpose built institution only involved in distance education.
2. Mixed-mode model. It teaches both conventional classroom based students and distance students. Mixed model systems are structured in different ways, the main ones are:
   (a) Separated distance teaching departments
   (b) Integrated distance education departments
   (c) Consortia

Some of the differences implicit in various models are explored in the various taxonomies of distance systems at higher education. Any particular taxonomy is wholly satisfactory because individual systems tend to exhibit different features in a variety of permutations.

A number of writers proposed model organizational structures for distance education systems. All these proposals assume a classic model or a separated distance unit undertaking all the functions associated with distance education.

Ram Reddy (1987), the founder of the open university system in India, suggested a model organizational structure for Indian open universities.

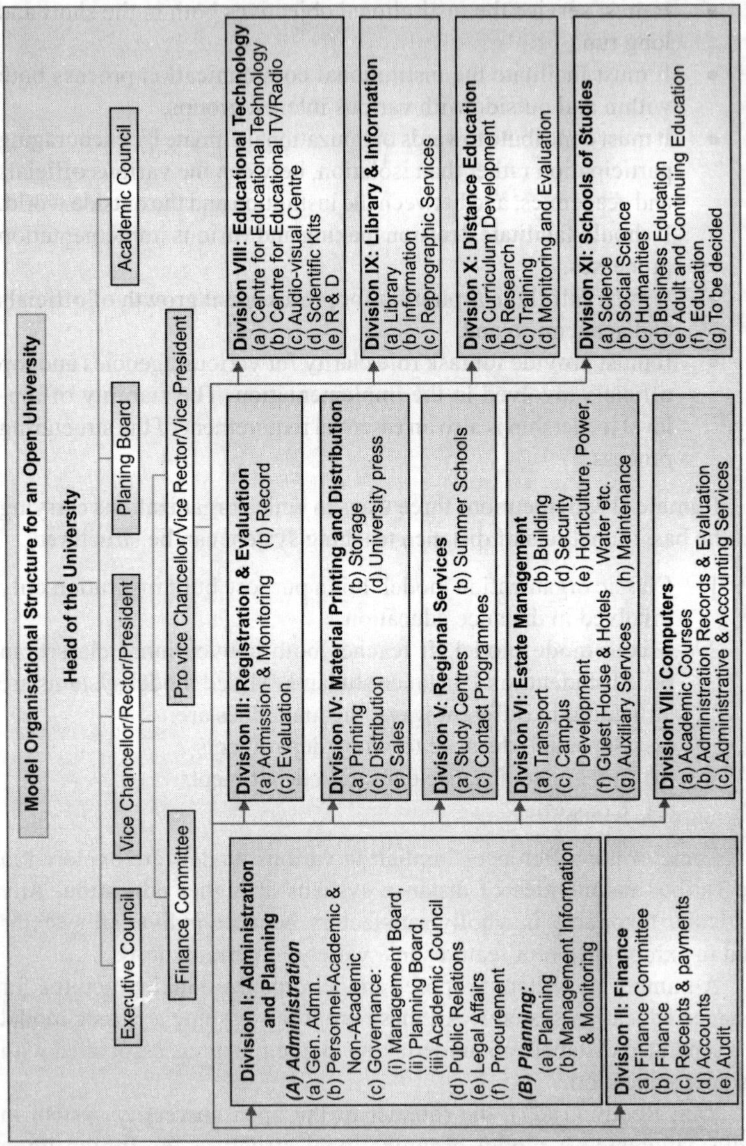

Model Organisational Structural of an Open University

8

Distance Education Programmes

A conventional university or a college, when newly established, would not experience any difficulty in launching academic programmes. It simply borrows or adopts the programmes of the previously established institutions. Normally, there is no need or scope for any experimentation or innovation.

A distance teaching institution, particularly higher level one, comes into existence not to generally duplicate the courses run by other traditional institutions. Its aim, goal, purposc and functions are different from a conventional institution. It has to foster and promote the educational development of a community in which it is located. Different sections of the community have different types of educational aspirations and needs. It has to educate the people who remain uneducated due to a variety of reasons—economic, social, cultural and historical. Distance teaching institution has a mandate different from that of conventional one. For instance, look at the aims of the Open University of Venezuela which are totally different from conventional universities in that country. The aims of the University reflected the nature of distance education it offered. The aims are:

- to offer real educational opportunities at the higher education level to students from different socio-economic classes in the society and especially to adults and those members of the working population who have not previously had the opportunity to attend a traditional institution
- to meet in part the social demand for higher education at a standard not inferior to those of the best higher educational institutions in the country.

- to contribute to the autonomous development of the country by meeting its needs for trained human resources, particularly in scientific and technological fields.
- to establish institutional structures and processes capable of continuous development and of incorporating innovations that will optimise the teaching-learning process.
- to develop a teaching-learning system relevant to the conditions, needs and aspirations of its students, and conducive to the stimulation of the students' capacity for creativity and critical thinking.
- to support the development needs of the nation in collaboration with other relevant agencies and institutions.
- to contribute to a significant diminution of unit costs in higher education.
- to provide its educational programmes throughout the country.
- to optimize the productive use of free time by persons following its programmes.

Considerations for Distance Education Programmes

The academic programmes offered by distance teaching institutions reflect both the underlying philosophies that brought them into existence and determine in part the kinds of students they attract. According to Rumble and Keegan (1982), the following four considerations seemed to have been particularly important in the academic planning of the distance teaching institutions, though some of them have, of course been influenced by more than one of these:

- the demand for trained personnel
- human capital theory
- the liberal Arts tradition
- the concern with lifelong learning

Types of Distance Education Programmes

Academic programmes offered by distance teaching institutes particularly, higher one, are differently categorized by different distance educators. One classification (Kaye, 1987) is:

- *Academic Programmes*: These are normally degree level courses. Many students enroll on these courses because of their need and desire for formal academic qualifications, either for personal reasons or employment changes.

- *Vocational Programmes*: Students enroll on these courses for specific job related reasons.
- *Recreational Programmes*: These do not aim at specific vocational needs and do not lead to marketable qualifications. But they aim at specific needs.
- *Basic Literacy and Numeracy programmes*: These are aimed at developing literacy among adults.

A former Pro-Vice-Chancellor of the UKOU, Ralph Smith (1987) classified distance courses into six broad categories:

- Training courses.
- Awareness courses.
- Updating courses.
- Academic courses.
- Conversion courses.
- Upgrading courses.

A former Vice-Chancellor of IGNOU, Kulandai Swamy, VC (1995) categorised the courses offered by an open university under six broad heads:

- Programmes that have no comparable courses in conventional institutions (Non-conventional programmes).
- Programmes of specific job relevance/job-orientation (Job-oriented programmes).
- Programmes of specific social-welfare orientation (Welfare-oriented programmes).
- Programmes seeking to cater to the unfulfilled or newly developed aspirations which may or may not have any immediate job-relevance to the learners (Programmes of life long education).
- Programmes seeking to update/upgrade the skills and qualifications of professionals and others with the focus set on an immediate job-oriented objective (Programmes of Continuing Education).
- Programmes which offer wider options of those within conventional system (Open Programmes for Conventional Students).

IGNOU offers more than 200 especially need-based academic, professional, vocational, awareness generating and skill-oriented programmes, leading to certificates, diplomas and degrees. The focus of the programmes are to meet the various academic and employment needs of the disadvantaged sections of the society. A number of programmes aim at meeting the requirements of counting education and training of people for professional growth.

IGNOU's courses are organized under following Schools:

 School of Agriculture (SOA)	 School of Computer and Information Sciences (SOCIS)	 School of Continuing Education (SOCE)
 School of Education (SOE)	 School of Engineering & Technology (SOET)	 School of Extension and Development Studies (SOEDS)
 School of Foreign Languages (SOFL)	 School of Gender and Development Studies (SOGDS)	 School of Health Sciences (SOHS)
 School of Humanities (SOH)	 School of Inter-Disciplinary and Trans-Disciplinary Studies (SOITS)	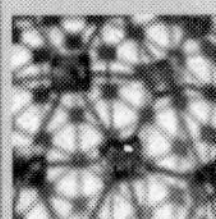 School of Journalism and New Media Studies (SOJNMS)
 School of Law (SOL)	 School of Management Studies (SOMS)	 School of Performing and Visual Arts (SOPVA)
 School of Sciences (SOS)	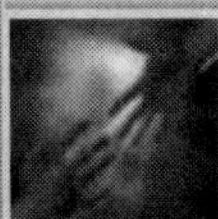 School of Social Sciences (SOSS)	 School of Social Work (SOSW)
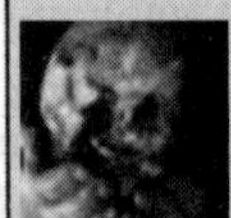 School of Tourism and Hospitality Service Sectoral Management (SOTHSSM)	 School of Translation Studies and Training (SOTST)	 School of Vocational Education and Training (SOVET)

Achieving Success from Distance Programmes

Some if not all, the following questions require an answer 'yes' if some degree of success is to be expected from any distant learning programme (Neil, 1981).

- Is there evidence of a significant public demand for the course and objectives proposed?
- Is there evidence of a need within the community for a course of the kind proposed?
- Is there some reasonable possibility of support for the project from agencies 'on the ground'?
- Is it clear that other agencies are not providing similar courses?
- Does the course offer some innovative or fresh approach to the subject?
- Is there likely to be a continuing demand?
- Is the course capable of development by other agencies?
- Is there an opportunity for the interested audience to pursue new interest aroused by the course?

Distance academic programmes must meet the following criteria:

- be useful for the labour market;
- be useful for social activities outside the labour market
- contribute to a scientific and/or cultural education;
- be attractive for large numbers of students;
- not exceed fixed cost;
- be appropriate for distant teaching;
- Alleviate the teaching capacity problems of existing institutions.

Preparation of Distance Courses

Course preparation in distance teaching institutions includes course planning and course development. Course preparation includes the production of radio and television programmes, audio cassettes, video tapes, discs, computer software and other non-print materials used along with print material. Here we mainly deal with print materials for distance learners.

Course Planning: Planning is the first stage and comprises the following steps:

- Assessment of needs
- Defining objectives
- Analyzing resources and limitations
- Selection of criteria from alternatives
- Development trials

- Evaluation/Assessment
- Feedback

***Course Development*:** The second stage in the process of course preparation is course development. Stone (1995) identified 4 approaches for course development.

- *Specialized Approach*: In this, various tasks involved in the development of materials are allocated to professional staff. Each specialist works on his own tasks, the analogy being with an assembly line.
- *Chain Approach:* In this, each specialist participates before and after his own task. This way the lack of integration of the specialist approach is overcome.
- *Interdisciplinary Team Approach*: Different specialists are brought together and given the collective responsibility of development of all materials.
- *Matrix Approach*: In this, project approved by appropriate specialists from functional departments are borrowed to perform specific tasks of the project. The head of each functional area maintains the responsibility for the quality of the work done by the specialist staff assigned to the project while the project manager has the responsibility for ensuring the completion of the project in a coordinated manner.

Models of Course Development

Mason and Goodenough (1981) described 5 course development models:

- Content specialist model
- Content specialist and editor model
- Content specialist and transformer model
- Instructional design model
- Course team model

These models are diagrammatically presented on the next page.

The content specialist model is relatively easy as content specialist can control the process of development. The teaching style and language will be consistent and uniform. The level of motivation to prepare quality product will be apparent. He will be able to adapt it to suit the learners and update it as and when required. There are also several disadvantages of this model. The content specialist may feel isolated. His work may be

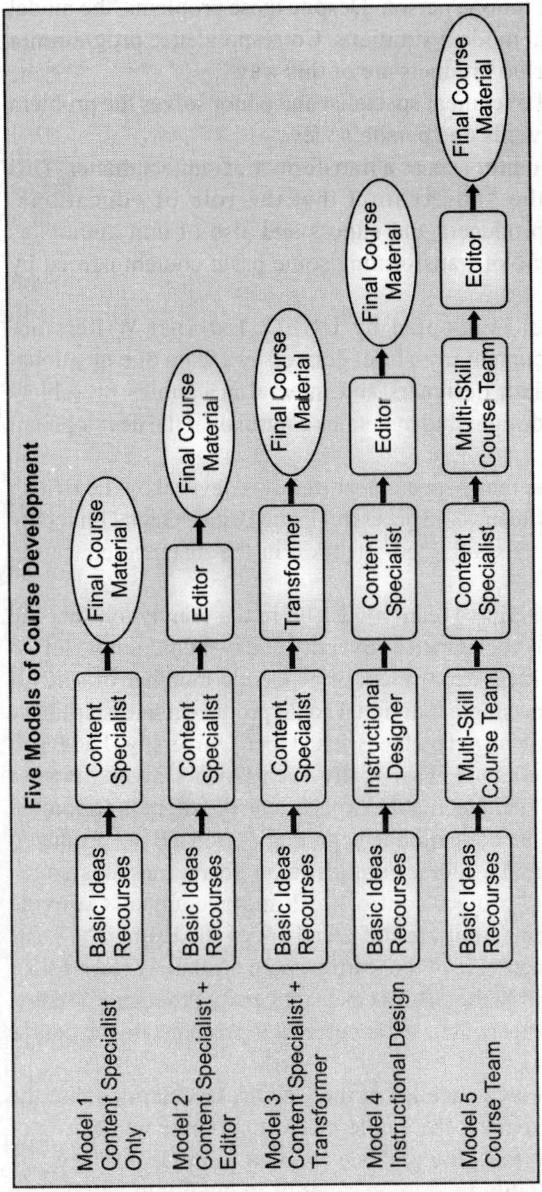
Five Models of Course Development
Model 1 Content Specialist Only
Basic Ideas Recourses
Content Specialist
Final Course Material
Model 2 Content Specialist + Editor
Basic Ideas Recourses
Content Specialist
Editor
Final Course Material
Model 3 Content Specialist + Transformer
Basic Ideas Recourses
Content Specialist
Transformer
Final Course Material
Model 4 Instructional Design
Basic Ideas Recourses
Instructional Designer
Content Specialist
Editor
Final Course Material
Model 5 Course Team
Basic Ideas Recourses
Multi-Skill Course Team
Content Specialist
Multi-Skill Course Team
Editor
Final Course Material

biased. The tasks of designing, preparing, checking and rewriting materials may be too much work for one person. Despite these problems, the model is adopted in some dual mode institutions. Correspondence programmes of University of Waterloo products are of this way.

The second model of content specialist and editor solves the problem of the first model. It avoids one person's view.

In third model an editor acts as a transformer of subject matter. This model is based on the "observation that the role of educational technologists, media producers and editors and also of unit authors as they polish drafts is one of transforming some basic content agreed by subject specialists".

The fourth model is adopted by UNED. External Writers are contracted to develop content from brief derived by a team of educational technologists, curriculum designers and internal academics or subject specialists. Thus team designs and maintains control over the development of courses.

The fifth model has many special features. It is devised by the British Open University. It has been very successful in the British Open University and because of this it has attracted attention in the distance education world.

The origins of the course team model lie in the conviction that the content and teaching of each Open University course could not be left to the whim of the individual department or academic member or staff. It was also believed that no single individual could produce interdisciplinary courses of the length envisaged by the British Open University. The result was the course team concept. Essentially each Open University team consists of a number of subject matter experts, one of whom is appointed course team chairman, an educational technologist, and a BBC producer, an editor, a staff tutor and a course administrator. Secretaries, designers, technicians, librarians, project control staff and accountants provide support in specialist fields but are not members of the team. The BBC producers, while full members of the team, remain ultimately responsible to their line manager within the BBC's Open University Production Centre, and the BBC formally clears their work before it is presented to the course team for approval.

Perry, the first Vice-Chancellor of the UKOU, has claimed that the concept of the course team is the single most important contribution of the Open University to teaching practice and that a course produced by this method will inevitably tend to be superior in quality to any course produced by an individual, but he has also admitted that it is an expensive way of developing materials and can only be justified if the materials are going to be used by large number of students.

According to North Cott (1978) the factors which favour the course team approach are:

- the project based nature of course development;
- the need to bring in educational technologists to help academics write good materials;
- the inter disciplinary nature of many of the early Open University courses;
- the need to integrate the broadcasts and printed materials;
- the size of the task, many people were needed to develop an Open University course in the timescales available; and
- the fact that innovation and creativity is encouraged by group interaction within course teams.

By and large the course team model

- needs a very democratic atmosphere,
- devotes a great deal of freedom and responsibility from the senior administrators to the members of each team.

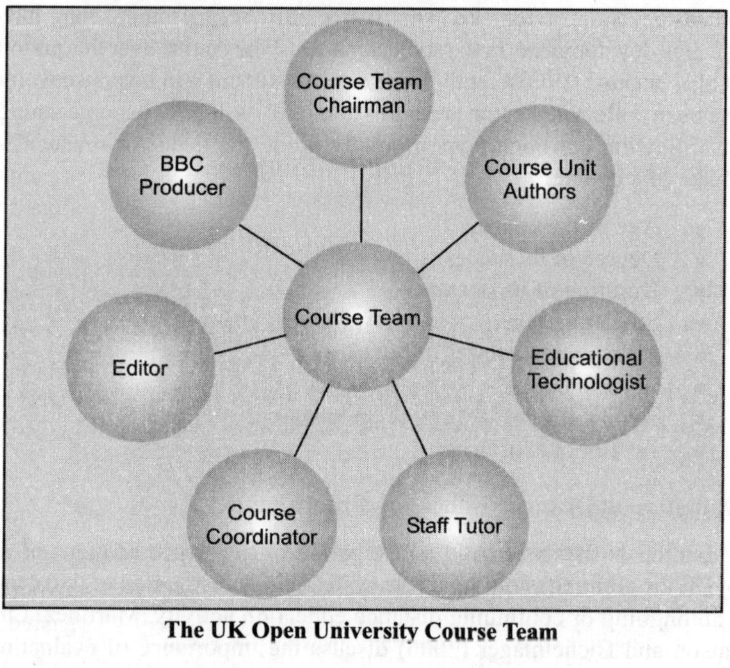

The UK Open University Course Team

- Contains an implicit assumption that academics will be able and willing to build up strong working relationships with each other and with other members.
- Requires academics to be employed full-time to ensure availability, commitment, coordination and continued maintenance to course once they are established.

From the academics view point there can be a number of problems with the course team model. Public scrutiny and discussions of work by peer groups and outsiders can be intimidating. It takes time for academics to learn to give and receive criticism and comment on the worth. Ideological conflict has to be carefully managed and resolved. A common problem is one of status, younger academics being unable or unwilling to discuss or change the work of more senior member of the team. By breaking these altitudes UKOU could operate this model.

Course Maintenance and Renewal

Maintenance of a course during its life and its eventual renewal or remake is as important as the original creation of the materials. Once a course has been offered for several years it is likely that considerable portion of it needs revision or remake. This is not only because there may have been new developments in the subject matter of the course over this period, but also because a sufficiently large data on student and response would have been collected that the pressures to modify will have become strong. The following considerations normally guide the need for revision or remake of a course:

- Age of the course
- Degree of its success
- Duration of its operation
- Stock position
- Life - expectancy
- Student body
- Availability of workforce on resources
- Institutional priority

Evaluation of Distance Education Programmes

Evaluation is the systematic investigation of the worth or merit of an object. Programme evolution is the systematic investigation of the worth of an ongoing or continuing distance education activity. Martinez, Liu, Watson and Bichelmager (2006) discuss the importance of evaluating distance education programmes. Evaluation of programmes is used to identify strengths and weaknesses as well as the benefits and drawbacks of teaching and learning online. They asked students, administrators and instructors to evaluate course management categories such as registration, support services, advising and sense of community. One important finding of the study is the equivalence of the distance education programme to the traditional programme information related to evolution and distance education is available in the works of Rossi, Lipsey and Freeman (2003), and Fetzpatrick et at (2004) and others.

Over the years, a number of experienced distance educators have developed evaluation approaches that focus exclusively on distance education. The work done in this area by Flagg (1970), Dunning et al (1993) Ehrmam (2001), Bates (2000) and Cyrs (2001) is representative.

Flagg focuses specifically on formative evaluation. He offers seven steps for planning and implementing a formative evaluation:

1. Clarity and state the purpose of the evaluation study.
2. Select and specify recipients of the evaluation information.
3. List evaluation questions.
4. Indicate the overall scheme of evaluation
5. Select data collection strategy and measurement tools
6. Identify respondent samples.
7. Select cvaluation setting and procedure.

Dunning *et al.* (1993) suggest that distance learning systems can and should be evaluated at three levels: the functional, the managerial and the instructional. Operationalizing distance education programme evaluation at these three levels, necessitates development of credible standards of quality grounded in benchmarks for learner satisfaction and achievement, instruction, student support services and integration of institutional values.

Ehrmann (2001) has contributed extensively to the literature on distance education evaluate. As the Director of the Flashlight Project (a programme of the American Association of Higher Educational Teaching, Learning and Technology Group) he spearheaded the investigation of evaluation issues from a variety of perspectives and has taken a leading role in developing a comprehensive 'Took Kit' to guide evaluators of distance education programmes. Using the metaphor of a Flashlight, which illuminates a small area brightly, he suggests that evaluators begin with a general, usually almost incoherent question of interest in one of these areas and then, transform it from a formless 'blob' to a focused evaluative 'triad'. He uses the 'triad' to refer to a focused question or set of questions crafted to examine (a) a particular technology or method in relation to (b) a particular practice enabled by that technology or method and (c) a desired programme outcome. The next step in the process is to ask questions in five related areas:

1. The technology per se
2. The use of the technology for the activity
3. The activity per se
4. Whether and how the activity is contributing to the desired outcome.
5. The outcome per se.

The Flashlight Project has developed a number of services and tools to help evaluators implement their own focused evaluation studies.

Cyrs (2001) offers evaluators guidelines for developing and implementing distance learning programme and course evaluations for audio, video, data, and print programmes. He focuses on 10 areas to guide evaluation of all forms of distance education.

Programme evaluation at the UK Open University is the systematic investigation of the merit of a particular distance education programme, curriculum, or teaching method and how it might be improved. As part of evaluation procedures for distance education by the UKOU (Woodley and Kirkwood, 1986), two alternative strategies have been merged. The first is the traditional, positivist-empiricist approach to evaluation. This represents as attempt to apply the rules and procedures of the physical sciences to evaluation. The second is more eclectic view of evaluation that incorporates qualitative and naturalistic techniques for the evaluation of distance education. The primary outcome of this type of evaluation is the comparison of the data collected from the tow into more categories of learners. For example, the distance learners are compared with these taught locally, and conclusions about the effectiveness of the distance education activity are made.

This approach represents the traditional process for the evaluation of distance education. Recently, a countermovement has emerged (House, 1996). It opposed traditional and quantitative procedures for evaluation. Now this way is incorporating more naturalistic methodologies with holistic perspectives. This perspective for evaluation uses focus groups, interviews, observations, and journals to collect evaluation information in order to obtain a rich understanding of events related to distance education activity.

From practical standpoint many evaluators now use a combination of quantitative and qualitative measures. According to Woodley and Kirkwood (1986), six categories of evaluation information can be collected about distance education activities:

1. Measures of activity
2. Measures of efficiency
3. Measures of outcomes
4. Measures of programme aims
5. Measures of policy
6. Measures of organizations

Woodley and Kirkwood summarize evaluation of distance education as being a fairly eclectic process that utilizes procedures that should match programme needs to evaluation activities.

Fortune and Keith proposed the AEIOU approach for evaluating distance education projects. It is similar to Woodley and Kirkwood's in that it is an eclectic one that uses quantitative and qualitative methodologies. It provides formative information to the staff about the implementation of their project. It also provides summative information about the value of the project and its activities. The AEIOU evaluation process provides a framework for indentifying key questions necessary for effective evaluation.

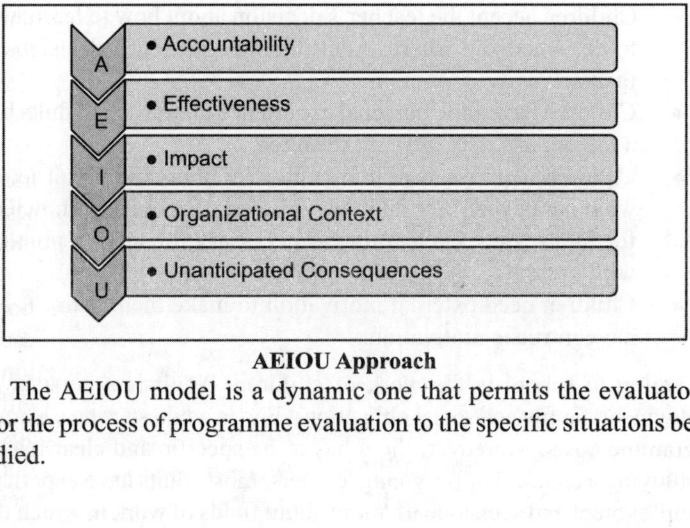

AEIOU Approach

The AEIOU model is a dynamic one that permits the evaluator to tailor the process of programme evaluation to the specific situations being studied.

9

Distance Students

Majority of distance education students are generally adults. Hence, an understanding of the nature of adult learning is useful for understanding adult learners. The best known description of adult learning is that of Malcolm Knowles (1978)

Knowles theory of adult education, what he called "andragogy" (the art and science of helping adults learn), can be reduced to the following propositions expressed as differences between adults and children:

- Children are dependent on teachers, adults are self-dependent and exercise personal responsibility.
- Children accept teacher's definition of what should be learned. Adult prefer to define it for themselves.
- Children accept the teacher's decision about how to learn, what to do, when and where. Adult like to make such decisions for themselves.
- Children have little personal experience to draw on. Adults have a lot and use it as learning resource.
- Children acquire a lot of information for future use. Adult acquire what is relevant here and now. Instead of acquiring knowledge for future, they see learning as necessary for solving problems with present.
- Children need external motivation to make them learn. Adults have intrinsic motivation.

Going to school is the work of children. Adult is a person with employment, family and social obligations. For an adult, starting a learning programme costs. Moreover, there has to be specific and clear reasons for studying a course. Unlike young learners, most adults have experience in employment and seek to learn more about fields of work in which they already know a great deal. Also unlike younger learners, adults know a lot about life, about themselves and about the world, about interpersonal relationships.

Some adults enroll in distance education courses:

(a) to compensate for a neglected high school education
(b) to seek college credits
(c) to improve their general knowledge
(d) to seek practical knowledge
(e) to improve employability, and
(f) to develop or upgrade the skills and knowledge needed in employment.

It is very difficult to list the topics that adult distant learners study, what is certain is that they cover about every subject under the sun. And whatever the reason for taking a course and whatever be the subject, it is also certain that adult distance students are always very serious, very committed and highly motivated about what they are doing. (Moore and Kearsley, 2005)

One aspect of distance education is that it has been studied from several different angles and involves factors that affect student success and failure. In most distance courses and programmes, a proportion of students who begin programmes do not complete them. In the past, high non completion rates were not unusual. Now a days, the rates of non-completion should be lower. One of the many difficulties in understanding dropout is usually a result of no single cause, but an accumulation and a mixture of causes.

In the area of distance and open learning, drop out has wider variation in its use. The study behaviour of distance students is different from that of campus based students and this alters drop out behaviours. The generally understood meaning of drop out would not hold good in distance learning context as it does not do justice to the various ways in which distance students drop out of their courses.

Kinds of Drop Outs

Fritsch categorized drop outs in distance learning into 5 groups:

Drop Outs in Some Distance Systems

Glatter and Wedell reviewed research around the world and concluded that drop out in distance courses is much higher than would be expected in full time courses and drop out rates vary with the length and types of courses.

1. Non-starters	• Students who enroll but who do not take up their studies in practice
2. Draw-backs	• Students who begin their studies but give up after the first attempts
3. Drop-outs	• Students who study regularly but who send in a few written assignments, or who are not successful in assignments and hence not allowed to appear at examinations
4. No shows	• Students who do not appear at examinations to which they are admitted
5. Failure	• Students who fail the examinations

A great deal of research has been done regarding drop out/attrition in various educational settings. Much of drop out research consists of descriptions of causal factors attained through empirical research. New conceptual models are now being evolved recognizing the complex interplay of variables which interact over a period of time to produce drop out. Some of these are narrow and some are wider, covering the interaction of student, institutional and environmental factors.

Why Drop Out?

Woodley and Parlett (1983) in their study of the U K Open University stated:

> "We have tried to take a system-wide look at student drop-out. This global approach has led us to consider general trends, patterns and explanatory models and to make suggestions for changes to the system as a whole. However, if we are to reach a more complete understanding of the drop-out process, we must complement the approach with more detailed micro analysis. On the individual student level we need to know far more about the psychological processes involved in becoming, then ceasing to be, an Open University student. By looking closely at individual courses and how students study them, we can perhaps make more detailed and concrete proposals for change."

In trying to understand why some students succeed while others drop out we must acknowledge the complex interplay of certain 'push' and 'pull' factors. 'Push' factors encourage them to continue while 'pull' factors lead to withdrawal. Below we give an over-simplified picture of the 'pull' and 'push' factors acting on an imaginary individual.

Push Factors	*Pull Factors*
Wants degree to get promotion.	Wants to spend more time with family.
Likes to finish something started.	Course is very difficult.
Very interested in the subject matter.	Fees are high.
Spouse is very encouraging.	Doesn't like course tutor.
Allowed time off for summer school.	Part time degree course available nearby.

Each of these factors will have different strengths and drop out will occur when the 'pull' factors barely outweigh the 'push' factors. Some students begin their course with the 'pull' factors and they are very vulnerable. In other cases the 'push' factors greatly exceed the 'pull' ones and it takes a dramatic new 'pull' factor such as a death in the family, or being sent abroad to work, to cause withdrawal.

Types of Drop Outs in UK Open University

Woodley and Parrett (1983) on the basis of statistical analysis identified in the following types of the UKOU students dropping out tendencies

- Very old and very young distance students are more likely to drop out. Men are more in danger of dropping out than women.
- The highest dropout rates can be found among distance students with manual jobs, the lowest among housewives.
- In general the danger of dropping out is greater when the level of previous schooling is lower.
- The highest dropout rates can be found among students living in London, the lowest among those living in the east Midlands.
- Students of mathematics and technology are more in danger of dropping out than students of the arts.
- The probability of dropping out is greater among those enrolled for older courses than among those enrolled for newer courses.
- If the recommendation was followed to work through another course for preparation before beginning the course, the dropout rate was lower.

- The more courses the students enrolled for, the higher the dropout rate.
- Courses with summer schools had fewer drop outs than courses without summer schools.
- The more teaching programmes in television and radio were bound with the course, the lower the dropout rate.
- The more literature (set books) was made additionally available, the lower the number of drop outs.

Contributory Factors for Drop Out

Woodley and Parlet (1983) listed several factors which can underlie drop outs from the UKOU students' perspective. Some of such factors are:

1. Course Factors

- Course found to be too difficult or not sufficiently advanced.
- Course required too many hours of study each week, i.e. 'over loaded'.
- Course badly designed and/or taught.
- Content found uninteresting,
- Content not as expected from the course description.

2. Institutional Factors

- Inadequate classrooms, equipment, parking, accommodation, etc.
- Administrative errors, e.g. not sent the teaching material.
- Required to leave by the institution.

3. Study Environment Factors

(a) *Unforeseen/unplanned changes*

- ➢ Personal/domestic changes such as illness of student or relative, change in marital status, having a baby, having to care for ageing relatives, moving house.
- ➢ Work changes such as increase in working hours or responsibilities, more travel, e.g. sent abroad, became unemployed, changed job, started work.
- ➢ Other changes such as withdrawal of financial support, loss of a quiet place to study, clash with other leisure activity.

(b) *Chronic factors*

- ➢ Little time or energy given to other domestic, work and leisure commitments.

- ➢ Lack of money.
- ➢ Lack of encouragement by spouse or employer.
- ➢ Transport problems.

4. Personal Blame

- I was too disorganized.
- I was not clever enough.
- I lacked the necessary study skills/background knowledge.
- I was too lazy.
- I lacked self-confidence.
- I had unreal expectations of the course.
- I couldn't face the assessment/exam.
- I took on too much along with my other commitments.

5. Motivational Factors

- Student no longer needs to complete the course as original goal have been achieved, e.g. gained promotion, learned something about painting.
- Original goal has changed, e.g. enrolled on course in order to become a teacher but now has decided to remain in present job.
- Goal met better elsewhere, e.g. student transfers to a course elsewhere which better meets his/her needs and circumstances.
- Realised goal would not be achieved, e.g. enrolled on class in order to meet people but did not get on with other students.
- Other goal has taken priority, e.g. student decides to spend more time on another hobby, trade union activities, voluntary work etc.

The Fern Universitat in Germany inquired several times into dropping out. A study in 1988 by Bartels, Prummer and Rossie revealed the following reasons for dropping out:

1 Change of job, job stress
2 Too much time required for studying
3 Restrictions on private life too great
4 The course would have lasted too long
5 Too much stress from family, household children
6 Would rather study at a campus university
7 Missed social contact with other students
8 Physical and mental stress too great

9 Could not find a working style suited to the system of the Fern Universitat
10 Expected more support from the Fern Universitat
11 Distance studies used as a preparation for possible place at campus university
12 Not enough success
13 No more support from family for distance studies
14 Have reached goal with the course
15 Course too difficult
16 Studying was not all that important for me
17 Had a different idea of what distance learning was
18 With everything connected with it, studying was too expensive for me

A number of researchers have developed formal models for predicting completion.

Kember (1975) presented a model for student progress that focused specifically on adult learners in distance education courses. The model focuses on the factors that affect a student's successful completion of a distance education programme with particular focus on the extent to which students are able to integrate their academic study with often conflicting employment, family and social commitments.

Kember's model suggests that students' entry characteristics direct them towards one of two pathways in a distance education course. Those with favourable situations tend to proceed on a positive track and are able to integrate socially and academically. Other students take a negative track where they have difficulties achieving social and academic integration, which affects their course achievement (GPA). The model also incorporates a cost/benefit decision step in which students consider the costs and benefits of continuing their study.

In the Billing's Model diagram (1988) the links represent the relationships among the variables. Billings found that students who made the most progress were those who had the intention of completing the course in a specific period of time, submitted the first lesson relatively early, had higher entrance examination scores and high GPA, had completed other correspondence courses, had a support of family, had high goals for completing the programme, lived relatively close to the instructor and had good college level preparation. The single most important predictor variable was the student's intention to complete, which suggests the importance of motivation over other factors.

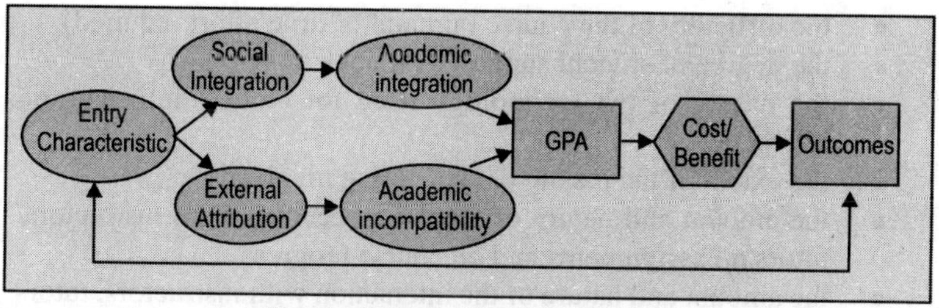

Kember's Open Learning Model

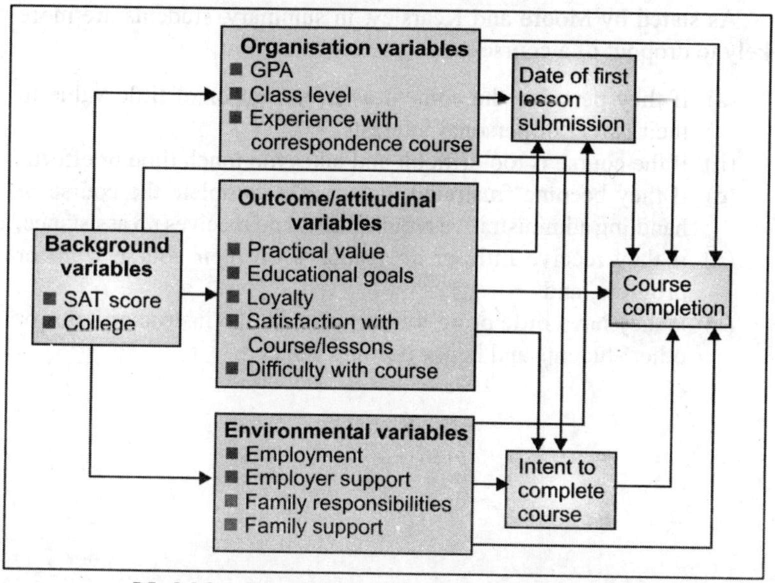

Model for Completion of Correspondence Course

Extra Curricular Concerns

A variety of extracurricular concerns, such as employment, family responsibilities, health and social interests can positively or adversely affect cooperation of distance courses.

Courses Concerns

Many features of the course or programme itself affect the success of students. These include (Moore and Kersley, 2005):

- the perceived relevance of the content to career or personal interests.

- the difficulty of the course (amount of time/effort required)
- the degree of student support available
- the nature of the technology used for course delivery and interaction
- the extent of the pacing or scheduling involved
- the amount and nature of feedback received from instructors/tutors on assignments and on course progress
- the amount and nature of the interaction with instructors, tutors and other students.

As stated by Moore and Kearsley, in summary, students are more likely to dropout of a course

(a) if they perceive the content as irrelevant or of little value to their career or personal interests,
(b) if the course is too difficult and takes too much time or effort,
(c) if they become frustrated in trying to complete the course or handling administrative requirements and receives no assistance,
(d) if they receive little or no feedback on their course work or progress, and
(e) if they have little or no interaction with the instructor, tutor or other students and hence become isolated.

10

Instructional System in Distance Education

A distinguishing feature of a Distance Teaching University (DTU) is its multi-media instructional system. Multi-media instructional system is mostly learner based, while the instructional system of a conventional university is teacher based. In this system teachers/ instructors are absent and students/learners are independent and mostly learn for themselves with the help of multi-media instructional packages. It is said that in a distance system the institution teaches where as in a conventional system the teacher teaches.

Broadly the instructional system of a higher DTU consists of the following:

1. Print
   - Self Instructional texts of lessons
   - Set texts
   - Supplementary materials
2. Broadcast Audio-Visual
   - Radio
   - TV
3. Non-Broadcast Audio-Visual
   - Audio-cassettes
   - Video tapes
   - Discs
   - Filmstrips/slides
   - Film/Film-loops
   - Computer systems

4. Practical/Project Work

- Home kits
- Laboratory experience
- Field work
- Computing

5. Inter-personal communication

- Correspondence tuition
- Telephone contact
- Tutorial classes
- Counselling sessions
- Self-help groups
- Residential courses

Instructional Systems of some Distance Teaching Universities

Distance Teaching Universities (DTUs) use a variety of media. The British Open University's Charter specifically enjoins it to advance and disseminate learning and knowledge "by teaching and research by a diversity of means such as broadcasting and technological devices appropriate to higher education". One of the objectives of the Indira Gandhi National Open University is "to advance and disseminate learning and knowledge by a diversity of means including the use of any communication technology..."

In fact, some of the open universities have titles signifying the influence and importance of communications technology. The prominent examples are: Japan's University of Air and China's Radio and Television Universities. Thus, a notable feature of distance teaching-learning system is "the planned use of a wide range of media.... suited to the needs of the students". The instructional systems of some major open universities would indicate the importance and role of various forms of communication media.

The instructional system of Open University of Israel consists of the following:

- Textbooks, specially designed and printed for EU courses
- Supplementary readings of various types
- Regular computer-marked and tutor-marked assignments and final examinations
- Television and radio broadcasts

- Teaching aids of many types including audio-cassettes, games and laboratory kits
- Centralized and regionalized library resources
- Organized tutorial sessions
- Regional study centers
- Organized study groups, often on employer premises or in teacher training colleges
- Tutoring by telephone
- Guidance and counselling services, particularly in self-study methods
- Field trips, workshops laboratory sessions

The instructional system of Allama Iqbal Open University of Pakistan consists of:

- Correspondence packages, which include self-learning printed texts and supplementary study material
- Radio and television broadcasts specially prepared for distance learners
- Tutorial instruction through correspondence and face-to-face teaching at Study Centers where possible, with workshops where appropriate
- Course assignments as an instrument of teaching and continuous assessment

The instructional system of the Open University of U K consists of:

- Course units—specially structured course books which form the core of the teaching material
- Radio and TV programmes—these are normally a relatively less important supplement to the course units although they form the part of the University's teaching which is best known to the public at large, (sometimes programmes are provided in the form of audio or video tapes).
- Assignments-essays or other written work—these may be marked by a Tutor (Tutor-Marked assignments TMAs) or by Computer (Computer-Marked Assignments CMAs).
- Examination—normally a three hour paper at the end of the course
- Residential School—either a one-week summer school or a residential week-end school
- Home experiment kit—these vary enormously according to the

type of course, e.g. rock samples for a Geology course, electric organ for a music course
- Computing—for some courses students require access to computer terminal facilities

The instructional system of Sukothai Thammathirat Open University of Thailand consists of:

- Correspondence texts, text books, workbooks, radio and television broadcasts, handbooks etc.

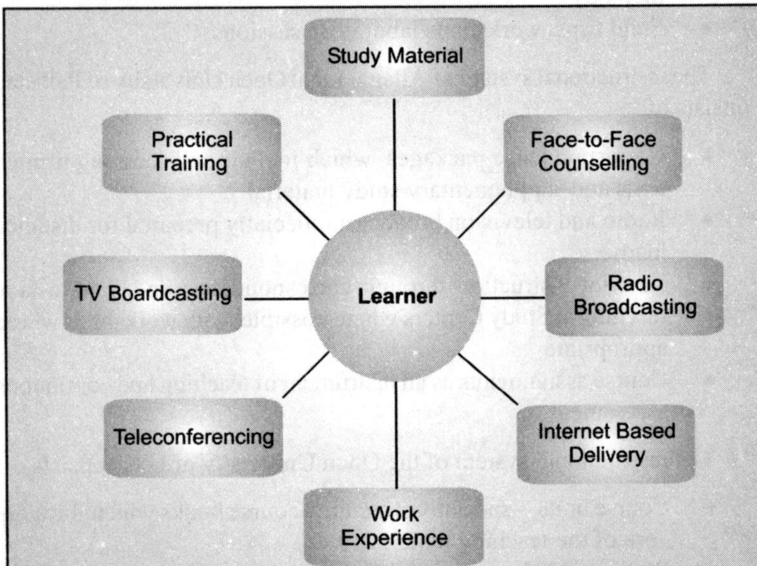

The learner-centric instructional system of IGNOU

The instructional system of Indira Gandhi National Open University consists of multi-channel, multiple media based teaching/learning packages. The different components used for teaching/learning include self-instructional print and audio-video materials, radio and television broadcasts, face-to-face counseling/tutoring, laboratory and hands-on-experience, teleconferencing, video conferencing, interactive radio counseling, interactive multimedia CD-ROM and internet based learning and the use of mobile phones for instant messaging. For courses in the sciences, computer sciences, nursing, medical sciences, education and engineering and technology arrangements are made to enable students to undertake intensive practice classes/practice teaching at select study centers/work centers/programme centers. While the traditional distance education delivery through print and study centre support is being strengthened, the university is strengthening the development of interactive multimedia content and learner support through video conferencing and web-based platform, by utilizing both Edusat and the Internet.

11

Self Instructional Material

Self Instructional Materials (SIM) are the main basis for distance teaching–learning. Teaching through SIM has been fast growing both in developed and developing countries. SIM in print is the dominant medium for distance teaching in all distance education institutions.

Conventional Class Room Teaching

In a conventional classroom the teacher transmits the content of the course and helps the students to absorb and use the contents. The teacher also helps students learn. In many ways the teacher helps student learning. The teacher

- arouses interest,
- develops motivation,
- makes objectives clear,
- attends to the difficult parts of the material,
- gives practice and feedback on the practice, and
- promotes two-way communication.

In distance education system students are away from the teachers. The teachers' role is performed by SIM. The various forms of support provided in classroom interaction are built into the SIM themselves. SIM thus become sources both of content and support.

SIM is totally different from normal textbook used by on-campus students. The difference between textbook and SIM is briefly summarised by Roger Lewis (1985).

SIM differ from textbooks and journal articles which are organized in terms of the subject matter rather than as aids to learning.

Difference between Textbooks and SIM

Textbooks	*SIM*
Assume interest	Arouse interest
Written for teacher use	Written for learner use
Designed for a wide market	Designed for identified groups
Rarely give objectives	Always give objectives
One route through	Many routes through
Structured according to logic of the content	Structured according to needs of learner
Little or no self-assessment	Major emphasis on self-assessment
Ignore likely learner difficulties	Address learner difficulties
Rarely offer summaries	Always offer summaries
Impersonal style	Personal style
Dense in content	Content unpacked
Densely packed appearance	Well-spaced-out appearance
Packaged for sale	Packaged for use
No mechanism to collect learner views	Learners' evaluation sought
No study skills advice	Provide study skills advice

Nature of SIM

Self instructional material are:

- self-explanatory
- self-contained
- self-directed
- self-motivating
- self-evaluating, and
- self-learning

Functions of SIM

- Help the individual learners find their way into and around the subject by repeating the content.
- Tell them what they need to do before tackling the material.
- Make clear what they should be able to do on the completion of the material.
- Advise them how to tackle the work.
- Explain the subject matter in such a way that the learners can relate it to what they already know.

- Encourage them sufficiently to make whatever effort is needed in coming to grips with the subject.
- Engage them in exercises and activities that make them work with the subject matter rather than merely read about it.
- Give the learners feedback on these exercises and activities enabling them to judge for themselves whether they are learning successfully.
- Help them to sum up their learning at the end of the unit.

To put it differently, SIM need to do the following:

- Get learners interested.
- Remind them of any necessary prior learning.
- Make clear what they will be learning next.
- Help them grasp the new ideas.
- Relate new ideas learners' own experience.
- Get learners think and do.
- Help them get constructive feedback on what they do.
- Adapt the teaching to each individual's needs.
- Enable them to reflect on their own progress.
- Help them build on what they have learned.

Special Features of SIM

SIM have many special features. Derek Rowntree (1992) stated the following special features of distance teaching materials.

- Clearly stated objectives.
- Advice about how to study the material.
- User-friendly, "You and I" style of writing.
- Short, manageable chunks of learning.
- Fewer words than usual per page (or screen)
- Plenty of helpful examples.
- References to the learners' experience.
- Illustrations used where they are better than words
- Headings to help learners find their way around.
- Links to other media where appropriate.
- Obvious awareness of different learners' needs
- Exercises that get the learners to use the material.
- Space for learners to write down their own ideas
- Feedback to help learners check their own progress
- Suggestions about getting help from other people.

Lockwood (1997) highlighted the following important attributes of self-instructional materials:

- Individual learning
- Self-paced learning
- Private learning
- Available at any time
- Available at any place
- Standardized text
- Expert content
- Updatable content
- Structural content
- Active learning
- Frequent feedback
- Explicit objectives
- Individualized tutoring

Learning Activeness

The chief characteristic of SIM is known as learning activeness. Materials are learner active, if they have the potential to interest learners to work and be involved in different types of academic activities such as noting the points, absorbing the concepts, collecting allied materials, applying what has been learnt to a new situation, doing self-check exercises, writing assignment responses and similar activities. Such built in strategies make material learner active and pedagogically meaningful.

Access Devices: Access devices are those devices which help the course writers go on to their learners as closely as they can, and help the learners come as close to the content as they can. These devices also help the learners find their way into the text. There are three main functions of these access devices.

- They enable learners to find what they need to read in the unit, i.e., the means and ways to reach the content.
- They make the content more intimate to learners and help them grasp what is presented in the unit.
- They perform the functions of a live classroom teacher i.e., build a teacher in the text.

Some of the access devices are:

- Title
- Structure of the Unit.

- Objectives.
- Division of content.
- Illustrations.
- Glossaries.
- Instructions

Developing Self Instructional Material

Self Instructional Materials (SIM) are the dominant medium of distance teaching in both developed and developing distance education institutions. Inspite of several advances in information and communication technologies and their impact on media of instructional system, print is widely used in all the distance teaching institutions. Special care is taken to ensure quality in the preparation of course materials. The course material should be self instructional so that the distance learner would be able to learn without the support of the teacher. In other words, the teacher is to be built into the material. There are many aspects and dimensions which should be considered while developing/writing SIM. SIM is normally divided into a number of units. There are many ways of writing a unit, but there are some features common to all. A SIM unit generally consists of three parts:

- Beginning of the Unit
- Main body of the Unit
- End of the Unit

Beginning of the Unit: This is the first part of the unit. It gives guidance on how to approach the unit and what to expect from it. Accordingly, this first part includes the following:

- Structure of the Unit
- Introduction of the Unit
- Objectives

Structure of the Unit: This is a detailed itemization of the content divided into sections and sub sections. It helps learners to overview the text and locate relevant parts easily. It exhibits structural relations with the contents. Some writers name it as contents. Structure is a better term in view of its pedagogical significance.

The structure makes the content more accessible to the learners. They can easily have access to the desired contents of the unit. They need not look through the entire content to find out the desired parts. It gives a clear outline of the content conceptualized by the unit writer. Structure with the help of clearly differentiated and logically and rationally arranged sections and sub sections make the unit more learner oriented. The section and sub-sections of a unit are numbered in simple manner. Each number conveys a meaning in terms of a unit or a section or a sub-section. E.g. 4.3.1 indicates 4th Unit, 3rd Section and 1st Sub-section. The titles of sections and sub sections should be clear, definite and relevant to the context of the unit.

Objectives: An objective is a statement of an intended outcome. It is a description of what the learner should be able to do after working on content. It is planned, observable and important. The emphasis on what the learner will be able to do lead to see that the most important part of an objective is the verb that begins it. It has to be specific enough to describe the behaviour that the successful learner follows.

Objectives serve the needs of a variety of people:

- They help writers to decide (a) what content to include (b) how to present the content and (c) what assessment questions to ask.
- They help counsellors to advise intending learners on what skills a course will develop.
- They provide basis for tutors to comment on learner assignments.
- They make it easier for all concerned to communicate: course planners with writers, writers with one another, planners with tutors.
- They help learners to see what skills a particular content intends to develop and whether or not these are relevant.
- They help learners to plan their work and to take on responsibility for their own learning and they help to check progress towards achieving the aim of the content.

Many courses require learners to cover a range of different objectives. It is to be checked that objectives succeed in this. Learners will often need to (a) acquire knowledge, (b) acquire skills and practice them and (c) develop particular attitudes. To put it other way, learners need to think, do and feel. The particular combinations of these kinds of objectives vary according to the course.

While stating objectives in behavioural terms, care needs to be taken in selecting appropriate verbs. Following are examples of such verbs used in stating objectives in behavioural terms:

Descriptive Verbs: define, describe, explain, write, name, list, select, state, etc.

Discriminative Verbs: compare, differentiate, identify, distinguish, give examples, summarise, breakdown, illustrate, outline, separate, select, etc.

Motor Performance Verbs: drive, type, draw, measure, write (learning how to write), etc.

Words like "know", "understand", "learn", "become aware of", etc. may indicate what the instructional objectives are i.e. what the institution or the course writer wants to happen after a particular unit is studied. But whether it happened or not won't be clear to the learner nor to the teacher as he cannot measure or see one's knowing, understanding, unless it is displayed by a corresponding behaviour. It is, therefore, necessary that the objectives in behavioural terms are stated. The following table helps transformation of objectives in instructional term to objectives in behavioural terms.

Objectives in Instructional Terms	*Objectives in Behavioural Terms*
Knows	Defines, describes, identifies, labels, outlines, reproduces, selects, states, lists
Understands	Converts, defends, distinguishes, estimates, explains, extends, generalizes, gives examples, infers, paraphrases, predicts, rewrites, summarise
Learns	Changes, computers, demonstrates, discovers, manipulates, modifies, operates, predicts, prepares, produces, relates, shows, solves, uses
Analyses	Breaks down, diagrams, differentiates, distinguishes identifies, illustrates, infers, outlines, points out, relates selects, separates, subdivides, categories
Synthesizes	Combines, compiles, composes, explains, generates, modifies, organizes, rearranges, revises, rewrites, summarizes, writes.
Judges	Appraises, compares, concludes, contrasts, criticises, describes, discriminates, explains, justifies, interprets, relates, summarizes

Introduction of the Unit: Introduction explains the content of the unit and links it with the preceding units and also with the current knowledge of the learner. It is brief and gives confidence to the learners that what they are going to study in the unit is manageable. Normally it has three components: (a) structural component, (b) thematic component, and (c) guidance component. Introduction contains some or all of the following:

- A statement of the course's objectives.
- An outline of the course contents.
- An indication of what previous knowledge students need, if necessary.
- A list of any equipment students will need such as a ruler, notebook, ledger paper, etc
- Advice on study habits, including advice on how to make use of supplementary media.
- Some remarks on conventions used in the text, such as key symbols, boxes and so on.
- Advice on other sources of help.
- Essential information about the examination for which students are preparing, if this is appropriate. This information should include a syllabus in some form details of how to register for the examination.

Main Body of the Unit

The Main body of the unit consists of the content in the form of sections and sub-sections each representing atleast one part of the content and self check questions related to the part. Normally each section relates to one objective of the unit. The body of the unit, thus, consists of a sequence of parts explaining a part and self-assessment questions, exercises and/or activities. Most need several hours of study and so learners cannot do so and in one study session. Therefore the matter is divided into sections. The content of a unit as a whole, needs to be conceptualized and worked out before writing. Working out the detailed structure is termed as "concept mapping". This is possible when the unit writer is thoroughly knowledgeable about the subject matter. The unit writer normally prepares more than one concept map concerning the concerned themes and selects the best of them.

After concept mapping, the unit writer takes into consideration while presenting the matter (a) small steps, (b) logical arrangement (c) sequencing, (d) personalised conventional style, (e) language, (f) illustration and (g) assessment.

The content is divided into the manageable chunks and each chunk is put under a section. The content is also logically arranged so that the learners proceed from one part to another. Each point is linked with the other so as to ensure logical arrangement.

Sequencing of the content is also important. The purpose of sequencing is to help learners tackle the content systematically and learn effectively. The sequencing is decided by the nature of the subject context. As per the subject requirement the sequencing is of four types: (a) chronological, (b) cause effect (c) flow chart/place to place, and (d) concentric circles. Irrespective of the types of sequencing there are a few principles of sequencing that are taken care of. These are: (a) concrete to abstract, (b) earliest to latest, (c) simple to complex, (d) known to unknown, (e) easy to difficult, (f) basic to advanced, (g) familiar to unfamiliar, (h) actual to representative and (i) special to general.

Personalised Style: SIM is to give a feeling for the learner that he is taught by a teacher who is not present physically. Generally learners are addressed by the word 'you'. 'We' is used when referred to ourselves. Writing SIM is to build a conversation between a teacher and a learner. The expressions are to be friendly and in conversational style.

Language: In writing SIM the points to be considered are: (a) paragraphing (b) sentences (c) vocabulary (d) negatives (e) passive and impersonal, (f) number of words and (g) means other than prose. Paragraphs need to be clearly structured. One idea is to be in one paragraph. Sentences are to be short and simply structured. Difficult ideas are easily understood that they are expressed in simple sentences. As far as possible, short, simple and formation words are to be used. Negatives are to be used with great care. Double negatives are particularly unhelpful. It is much easier to absorb a negative than a positive emphasis. Passive voice and impersonal usages are to be avoided, wherever possible. Means other than prose should be used wherever possible. Lists, graphs and the other visual devices can be used wherever possible.

Illustrations: Illustrations provide pictorial support to writing. They should have educational value. They should not dominate the content of the unit. They should be simple and self explanatory and should be directly linked with the content of the unit. They should be recognizable. Illustrations are of various kinds (a) lists, (b) word diagrams, flowcharts, logical trees, (c) tables, (d) graphs, (e) time lines, (f) cartoons, (g) diagrams, (h) photographs, (i) symbols, (j) pie charts, (k) block graphs, and (l) bar charts.

Assessment: In a well run conventional class the teacher asks questions to arouse interest of the learners. The learners themselves put questions to teachers to get their doubts clarified and to seek other help.

The teacher gives the learners the chance to check their own progress and also guides the learners and provides feedback to students. The situation for distance learners is difficult. They are away from teachers. They learn mainly on their own, in isolation from teachers and fellow learners. They cannot get the help from teachers. The course package has to guide the learner and to indicate to them how well they are doing and progressing. The course writer can (a) ask questions that arouse interest of the learners and prepare them for the study of particular topic, (b) provide questions which give learners the chance to check for themselves how well they are meeting course objectives, (c) provide feedback in the form of answers and discussions, and (d) include activities that enable learners to assess their new skills and knowledge levels. In SIM two types of assessment are used. Self-assessment questions (SAQs), exercises, activities and assignment questions constitute one type. The second type consists of term end examination, which exclusively measure learners' performance.

Writing SAQs is not easy. Lewis (1985) provided the following guidelines for writing SAQs:

- They should relate to course objectives.
- They should be inviting to the learners.
- They should be realistic in the demands they make.
- They should be varied type in the length of answers required.
- They should be frequent.
- They should make clear for the learner exactly what is required.
- Writer should provide any study advice necessary to help the learner to answer.
- They should be sign posted visually and in accordance with an agreed convention.
- They should be followed by answers or responses.

Activities: Like SAQs activities also are very helpful and have pedagogic value. They provide opportunity to learners for practice of knowledge gained through the SIM. Activities mean things that have to be practically done. They encourage learners to relate the text material with practical experience. As such they may not have model answers at time. Under the activities the course writer (a) can direct the learners for educational materials or (b) advise them to go on a study tour to collect information, or (c) suggest to our experiment, etc.

Exercises: Exercises are different from activities. They facilitate learning, through practice and reinforcement. Through exercises, learners will be able to check or revise their performance and retain information.

Assignments: Assignments are of two types mainly, TMAs and CMAs. Description of assignments is given in a separate chapter.

End of the Unit: The last part of the unit has components of summary, glossary and suggested books and articles. As a part of the unit, the important points of the unit are summarized. It provides feedback and recollection to the learners. It provides recapitulation and reinforcement. Summary can be in the form of a check list. It also can be in the form of list of key points that are covered.

Glossary helps learners comprehend the concepts discussed in the text. Glossary is not compulsory. It depends on the nature of the content - such words should be glossed which need elaboration for better comprehension. Glossary also becomes necessary when new concepts are introduced in the unit.

Suggested books and articles: Many courses may need learners to

Design of SIM unit

Unit No.	*Structure*		*Title of the Unit*
x.0	Objective		
x.1	Introduction		
x.2	Section 1 (Main Theme)		
	x.2.1	Sub-section 1 of Section 1	
	x.2.2	Sub-section 2 of Section 2	
	....		Check your Progress
	....		
x.3	Section 2 (Main Theme)		
	x.3.1	Sub-section 1 of Section 2	
	x.3.2	Sub-section 2 of Section 2	
	....		Check your Progress
	....		
x.4	Section 3 (Main theme)		
	x.4.1	Sub-section 1 of Section 3	
	x.4.2	Sub-section 2 of Section 3	
	x.4.3	Sub-section 3 of Section 3	
			Check your Progress
x.5	Let us Sum Up		
x.6	Glossary		
x.7	Suggested Books, Articles, Tapes, Reference, etc.		
x.8	Model answers to Check your Progress questions.		

read additional materials. Suggested books and articles should be useful to the learners as well as easily available.

Answers: Answers to SAQs need to be prepared at the end of the unit. For easy reference, the model answers need to be numbered the way they corresponding questions are numbered.

Evaluation of Self Instructional Material

Evaluation is the process of getting various peoples' views/reactions to SIM, with a view to improve them. It is getting feedback about the acceptability and the effectiveness of materials. Evaluation can lead to noticeable improvements in students' learning. Evaluation of materials is done in three ways.

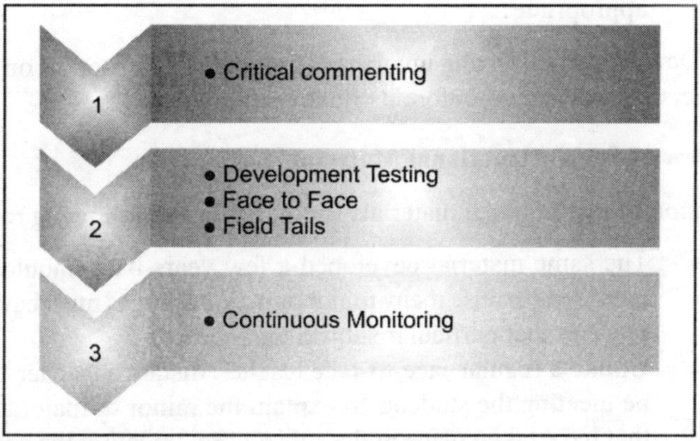

Critical commenting on material is to be done by subject experts, tutors and recently passed out students. It should be on subject matter well as teaching effectiveness.

On subject matter, the following questions are to be put and answered:

- Are objectives sufficiently explicit?
- Are any additional objectives to be added?
- Is content appropriate to objectives?
- Is subject correct and up-to-date?
- Is there any redundant material?
- Is material given logically?
- Does it avoid over simplification and over generalization?
- It is balanced and careful to recognize opposing viewpoints where appropriate?

- Does it give inappropriate examples?

On teaching effectiveness the following questions are to be put and answered:

- Will learners understand what is expected of them?
- Will learners have any difficulty in achieving any of the listed objectives?
- Is material pitched at the right level of intended learners?
- Do the examples seem relevant to learners' interest?
- Do you suggest any additional examples?
- Are all new terms fully explained?
- Are SAQs meaningful and appropriate?
- Does assignment or suggested follow up activity seem appropriate?

Developmental testing involves in trying out the materials on sample learners and revising it before its final version.

Review of Self Instructional Material

Revision of instructional materials is crucial for the following reasons:

- The same material developed a few years back should not be provided because many minor or major changes must have taken place in that particular subject area
- Unlike a regular face-to-face teacher, distance teacher will not be meeting the students to explain the minor or major changes that have taken place in the subject. So, updating the content is not possible.
- The only alternative in such a situation is the revision of material periodically, if not frequently.

The following need to be considered before revising the material:

- Age of the course material
- Degree of its success
- Its stock position
- Its life expectancy
- Strength of students for the course
- Financial resources
- Availability of human resources
- Institutional priority

12

Student Assignments

A student assignment for submission holds a central position in distance education. "It is probably the single most important mechanism for prompting and for pacing the individual's study and offers the only vehicle available to all students for feedback and dialogue with a tutor about their individual progress".

Importance of Assignments

Assignments enable students to test how effectively they have been studying their courses. Through them students receive evidence about their own progress and guidance to improve it. They constitute a dynamic tool for a dialogue between the teacher and the students. They invite active and meaningful participation of the students and provide a tool for monitoring progress and assessing achievement. According to Mackenzie *et al.* (1971) this was the only thorough going and substantial method open to the student to develop and promote his thinking. According to Lewis (1985) assignments for submission give learners an opportunity to converse with the tutor, to receive advice on their problems and to confirm their understanding of the problem. Through the assessed assignments the distance teacher is able to check the students' progress and assess their strengths and weaknesses. Lewis further pointed out that assignments enable the tutor to consolidate a relationship with the learners and the teaching institution to obtain feedback on the course as a whole. In a way they compel students to read the materials and therefore promote active learning beyond the passive reading of the course material. The importance of assignments as an integral part of distance teaching-learning is evidenced by the fact that they constitute up to considerable percent of the final grade in courses of many distance education institutions. They constitute up to 50 per cent of the final score of courses in the British

Open University and up to 30 per cent in Indira Gandhi National Open University.

Functions and Purposes of Assignment

Assignments, as mentioned above, serve a variety of functions. According to surveys conducted by the European Correspondence Schools and the British Open University (Baath, 1980) they:

- give students effective feedback through which students correct their mistakes and control their progress
- motivate the students
- enable teachers to evaluate student's achievements during the course, so that they can give each student help
- provide the opportunity for tutors to motivate students by giving them encouragement and praise.
- activate the students
- give students opportunities for application and transfer of their knowledge.
- focus the student's attention on important learning objectives
- develop the methods of retaining knowledge and the practice
- enable students to revise the whole study units.
- provide opportunities for students to develop skills in survey, summing up and integrating various parts of units.
- compel students to develop regularity of work.
- create opportunities for contacts between teachers and students thereby counteracting student's feeling of isolation.
- Assignments, according to Phil Race, serve several useful purposes. They help learners prepare for formal exams (where relevant).
- give learners feedback comments on their work, and develop their self-confidence
- give learners a measure of how successful (or otherwise) their work is.
- form basis for communication between learners and their tutors.
- provide learners with deadlines and stages to help them structure the timing of their work.
- maintain and develop learners motivation and commitment to their studies.

Types of Assignments

Assignments are broadly two types:

- Tutor Marked Assignments (TMAs)
- Computer Marked Assignments (CMAs)

Tutor Marked Assignment has several forms:

- Open and Unstructured Essay
- Structured Essay
- Role play Essay
- Interpretation of Data
- Design
- Project
- Description of process
- Notes
- Definition
- Hypothesis
- Calculation
- Sketch
- Critical Review

Computer Marked Assignment too has two broad forms:

1. Those where everything is given	*2. Those where learner must supply*
• Multiple choice • Matching • True/False • Putting points in a sequence or hierarchy • Blank spaces with words • Drawing a graph	• One word • List • Phrase • Sentence • Paragraph • Plan • Case study with questions • Drawing a graph • Practical

Preparing Assignments

Assignments are to be prepared very carefully and cautiously as they are the important channel of teaching and learning at a distance. Some of the guidelines provided by experienced distance teachers to properly write assignments are:

- they should relate to course objectives.
- they should be inviting to the learner.
- they should be realistic in the demands they make.
- they should be varied in type and in length of answer required.
- they should be clear and well structured.
- they should have study advice, if necessary.
- they should be appropriately phased.

The following checklist of criteria for the design of useful assignments questions is given by Phil Race.

- Is the question clear and unambiguous?
- Does the question directly relate to stated learning objectives?
- Have learners been adequately prepared for the question?
- Are there several ways of answering the question properly?
- Does it prepare learners for the sort of question that may be met in formal assessments or exams?
- What is the main purpose of the question (for the learner) or feedback?
- If the assignment is to be used for assessment, can learners tell how many marks go with each question?
- Will it be useful to prepare a model answer (or answers) to issue to learners along with feedback?
- Does the assignment as a whole test the main things the learner needs?
- Does the assignment begin with fairly easy questions?

Ways in which Tutors Teach through their Written Comments on Assignments

In many ways written comments are used by tutors. According to Rowntree (1992) they:

- draw the learners' attention to facts they have overlooked or misinterpreted.
- Suggest alternative explanations or interpretations.
- guide learners on the handling of evidence.
- show how to use quotations from texts.
- draw attention to gaps in the learners' reasoning.
- suggest how learners might present their ideas more effectively.
- offer new data that will help learners extend their understanding.
- ask for further explanation of muddled answers.

- demonstrate short-cuts in problem-solving.
- draw attention to how a piece of work might have been improved, e.g. in content, balance or logic.
- point out relationships between the learners' present work with their earlier work.
- commend the learners for any unexpected insights, special efforts or improvement in skills.

Types of Tutor Comments

Comments of a distance teacher on the assignment responses of a learner help the learners (a) to sustain interest in learning, (b) to get motivated and activated, (c) to facilitate learning, and (d) to assess his progress in comparison with others. Tutor comments, therefore, should be necessarily of teaching type. If they are not of teaching type, they defeat the purpose of teaching-learning at a distance. Distance teaching-learning is more successful when the non-contiguous two way communication is frequent and constructive. In a conventional marking the teacher tries to find out mistakes. In distance learning evaluation, the teacher not only finds out mistakes, but, also writes constructive and meaningful comments suggesting a student (a) his learning style (b) level of performance (c) limitations and (d) how to overcome limitations for better performance.

Tutor comments can be broadly classified into 2 kinds:

1. Non-Teaching Comments	*2. Teaching Comments*
• Harmful	• Positive comments
• Hallow comments	• Constructive comments
• Misleading comments	• Global comments
• Null comments	• Personal comments
• Negative comments	

Assignment Turn Around Time

"Turn around time is the time from the moment the student mails in the homework assignment for a study unit until it is received by the student with the tutor corrections and comments. The assignment turn around time is of great concern and a sensitive matter. The problem of long turn around time of assignments appears to affect many distance education systems in the world. The importance of the turn around time is empirically supported by many studies. In distance learning long turn around time would have unfavourable effects on students' motivation. "Nothing is more disheartening to the student than to put forth the efforts necessary to prepare an assignment and then wait and wait for its return". Harter's investigation revealed that the most frequent reason for dropping out given by the student was that they had to wait too long for the return of their assignments. International studies have shown that turn around time varies from 1 to 90 days. Mackenzie et. al (1971) found that many students at the British Open University generally complained about long turnaround time although they appreciated their tutors' comments on assignments. Another study done in 1987 at the British Open University showed that, on average, it took a waiting time of 24 days for a student to get each marked assignment.

According to Holmberg (1986) the obvious weakness in normal distance study is that feedback is delayed because of the slowness of the communication process characteristic of this type of education. He states:

> "For a student assignment to be sent by the student, received by the supporting organization, corrected, commented on and returned to the student so that he/she receives it with a week is considered remarkably quick and represents a turn around time that many distance education institutions seem unable to achieve."

A recent Australian project on assignment turn around time investigated educationally effective and cost effective methods of reducing turnaround time. The investigation focused on three issues: (1) factors contributing to delays in turn around time (2) means of reducing turn around time while maintaining desirable standards and (3) educationally effective and cost effective application of technologies to reduce turn around time: The project highlighted the effect of feedback on the way students perceived themselves, the course personnel and the university as a whole. Where return was handled efficiently students' morale and confidence were boosted... conversely anxiety, dissatisfaction and even hostility were generated by tardiness

Students' Perspective of Correspondence Tuition

A research study of British Open University by Cole, Coats and Lentall (1986) highlighted what students want from correspondence tuition. The following are desired by distance learners (Robert, 1996):

- to have their work treated with respect from an instructional point of view, to get the grades necessary to pass the course.

- fair and objective grading.
- an explanation and justification of the grade.
- to know the significance of the grade (eg. that 'C' is a good solid grade) and when letter grades are used, to know where they come within the grade and if there has been an improvement even if the grade is the same.
- a clear indication of how they can improve both in terms of the specific question and more generally. This is particularly important to students who feel stuck in a grade.
- a sympathetic, friendly and supportive approach, indicating that the tutor is 'on their side'.
- not to be talked down to or patronized.
- encouragement and reassurance about their own ability, but balanced with honesty.
- positive comments and not simply negative, critical ones.
- specific comments (eg indicating clearly the strengths and weaknesses of the assignment, giving useful references) not vague generalities.
- constructive criticism and advice (eg. not simply to be told that they have gone wrong but in what way and what to do about it, direct references to the course material to indicate references to the course material to indicate where to find what they have missed/misunderstood etc.).
- full comments (in particular on the script itself) since these can be of value not only at the time but for revision purposes in the case of the stronger student, to be challenged.
- not just congratulated, clearly expressed and legibly written comments - not complex, confusing or unreadable advice.
- an opportunity and invitation to respond (e.g. at tutorials, phone).
- a quick turn around to get one TMA back before the next is due.

Monitoring of Assignments

The work of commenting, grading or marking assignments needs to be monitored for ensuring effective distance teaching-learning. Monitoring serves many purposes:

- uniformity of marking standards.
- feedback to part-time staff on the work they are doing.
- feedback to course teams on students' progress on their work.
- rescheduling assignments.

- reducing/Increasing the number of assignments in the course.
- modifying the advice and guidance given to learners on how to answer.
- changing the tutor notes.
- Modifying the course material.

Monitoring system is prevalent in all the developed distance teaching institutions. One of the aspects of the British Open University teaching system frequently praised is the monitoring system. In this system, samples of each tutor's marked scripts are reviewed by full time academics responsible for course presentation or for tutor appointments and supervision. Monitors write reports on the tutors' work and these reports are communicated to tutors in a variety of ways via staff tutors in the Regional Centers of the University. The system provides opportunity for rendering an academic's teaching visible to another; thus enabling staff to learn from each other's work and advice. Each Academic Faculty of the University has its own monitoring procedure.

Nature of Monitoring Comments

In general, monitoring comments should be positive, constructive and supportive if they are to enhance performance. This would include according to Cole, Coats and Lentell (1986):

- linking comments to tuition skills and not simply to academic content. Remembering that the role of the correspondence tutor is to help the student to improve, comments should embrace all aspects of teaching and not just the handling of content, for instance, this might include commending the relationship the tutor is seeking to establish, the tone of the tutor's comments etc;
- commending and reinforcing the strengths of the tutor's teaching — not simply picking up on any deficiencies;
- giving positive guidance where appropriate e.g. showing how the tutor might have handled teaching the student a particular point or skill;
- explaining and clarifying evaluative comments e.g. not just passing judgments but indicating why a grade or a point is inappropriate;
- making reasonable and realistic demands which are likely to lead to improvement and not be regarded as excessive or exploitive;

- generally showing respect for the tutor's professional skill, judgment and knowledge. This might include adding supportive comments such as, I am sure this student will benefit from your skill/expertise.

Assessment of student learning through assignments is solely for the benefit of student. Yet, there are a number of stakeholders in the assessment process and it meets a complex and interwoven series of needs. These needs can be grouped into four:

- Students' needs
- Teachers' and trainers' needs
- Institutions' needs
- Community needs

13

Student Support Services

The separation of teacher and student is a basic characteristic of distance education. The role of the conventional classroom teacher is performed by the self-instructional materials (SIM) in distance teaching. SIM are self-explanatory, self-contained, self-directed, self-motivating and self-evaluating.

Problems of Distance Learners

Research and practice of distance learning indicated that self-instructional print and non-print materials are not fully supportive of distance learning, because they fail to solve several of problems faced by distance learners.

The problems faced by a distance learner are broadly classified into three kinds:

- Problems relating to study techniques and learning difficulties,
- Problems arising from interaction with a remote and impersonal institution, and
- Personal problems which affect the student's work.

Another way of classifying them is as barriers at many stages of a student's progress, such as:

- Study related barriers
- Time related barriers
- Institutional barriers, and
- Personal barriers

The problems faced by distance learners include:

- Physical and intellectual isolation of learners from the teaching institutions, teachers and fellow students. This often leads to frustration and eventual dropout.

- Delay in feedback to students' communications and assignments
- Methods of instruction novel to the majority of learners. This leads to delayed adjustment to the content, which may lead to delayed learning
- Competing interests for the learners time and attention
- Limited access to additional reading and library facilities due to difficult geographical locations. This leads to over-dependence on correspondence notes.
- Family, peer, local community and social attitudes may often be biased against distance education in favour of the conventional mode, leading to depression, and eventually persuading the learner to drop out of the programme.
- Sometimes learners lack confidence in themselves and in the distance learning system.
- In cost sharing, some learners lack sufficient finances to pay towards their own education, in addition to supporting their children and those from the extended family.
- To many learners, a distance education mode of delivery is new. As a result learning becomes largely theoretical and therefore more difficult.

Though distance study is mainly a form of independent study, it is not and should not be sentenced to solitary confinement. Increasingly distance teaching institutions are acknowledging that their students need support beyond what is provided by teaching staff and teaching materials. The quality, quantity and efficiency of student support are significant in distance teaching institutions.

In emphasising the need to provide adequate academic support to distance learner, Perraton states that, "No matter how good our teaching materials and how efficient our distribution system, distance students have to work by themselves without the support that comes from tutors… we need to consider how we can give them the individual encouragement, help, tuition and guidance which they may need to overcome the barriers and distance and the remote students' feeling of isolation"

Ormond Simpson (2002), the Director of the UKOU Centre for Education Guidance and Student Support classified student support into two broad areas. The first is academic (or tutorial) support which deals with supporting students with cognitive, intellectual and knowledge issues of specific courses or set of courses. This includes, for example, developing general learning skills, numeracy and literacy. The second is non-academic (or counselling) support which deals with supporting students in the effective and organisational aspects of their students. There are further subdivisions within these two divisions.

Academic Support consists of:

- defining the course territory
- explaining the concepts
- exploring the course
- feedback-both informal and formal
- developing learning skills-numeracy and literacy
- chasing progress-following up students' progress through the course
- enrichment-extending the boundaries of the course and sharing the excitement of learning.

Non-Academic Support Consists of:

- advising-giving information, exploring problems and suggesting directions
- assessment-giving feedback to individual on non-academic aptitudes and skills
- action-practical help to promote study
- advocacy-making out a case for funding, writing a reference
- agitation-promoting changes within the institution to benefit students
- administration-organising students support

Composition of Student Support Services

There is no well established system of student support in distance education. It varies from institutions to institution. Many factors contribute to the development of a student support system. As David Sewart, as the outgoing President of ICDE in his keynote address at the 16th ICDE world conference stated, each student support system represented in any distance teaching system is unique and what is provided in it depends on the market, aimed at, the package which is employed, the delivery form, the status of the organisation and the socio-economic educational culture in which it operates. Student support services encompass a broad field and include admissions, registrations and records; examinations; information services; advising and counselling; and student advocacy and instructional support services. According to Sewart the support services in most distance education institutions include some or more of

- class teaching at study centre

- individual tutorials at study centres or other locations
- annual residential schools (compulsory or optional)
- study of self help groups
- social events
- counselling sessions at study centre
- correspondence with tutor and counsellor
- telephone contact with tutor and counsellor
- group telephone tutorials
- radio tutorials
- audio cassette correspondence
- computer mediated communication
- student newspapers

The popular and important forms of student support services are:

- Information support
- Guidance support
- Counselling support
- Tutorial support
- Library support

British Open University Model of Student Support

The British Open University developed a rich structure of student support services which was in many ways the central innovation of the system. The system is a link between materials and learning and has the following nine interlocking components which are described by Sewart (1978) as a "continuity of concern for the students studying at a distance".

- the tutor-counsellor who follows the student throughout his/her university career,
- the tutor available for consultation on an individual course,
- 13 regional offices providing a decentralised focus for the administration of tuition, counselling and student support systems,
- a study centre within easy travelling distance where the student can meet other students and use facilities,
- tutorials at regular intervals,
- computerised student records that can pick up problems in student's progress and anticipate drop-out
- Kosmat analysis - a computerised weighting of the grades given by tutors on all assignments against the national average,

- residential summer schools, and
- a student association with regional branches.

It is difficult to make comparisons across institutions in terms of the kinds of student support services because the terms 'informing', 'advising', 'guiding', 'tutoring', and 'counselling' are often used interchangeably or with overlap of meaning. However, how they are provided within a system can be known through the examination of the important roles of tutors, counsellors and local centres in student support services.

Should Support Services be Mandatory for Students?

Of late, a case is made by Brindley and Jean Louis for making selected student support services mandatory for distance students. They argue that too many students in distance education do not take advantage of student support services available to them. This results from either a lack of awareness that such services exist or from a failure to recognise the benefits that such services provide. They contend that the consequences of distance education students failing to avail themselves of such services contribute to exercising high rates of drop out. In brief they argue that an 'interventionist' role is necessary in which selected student support services would become mandatory. The suggestions of Brindley and Jean Louis are opposed by many. Thompson says 'we must be conscious of evidence suggesting that some students are attracted to distance education programmes because of the autonomy and independence that it offers. Such students might be deterred by programmes with compulsory participation in student support services that they judge to be unnecessary and unwelcomed'.

Information Support

Distance learners require many types of information about the institution they are studying with. In countries where the educational development level is low, the information requirements of distance learners are many and varied. In a conventional system of education, students need very minimum information, whereas in distance education which separates teachers from students, several types of information are required by students. Information is required before entering the institution and as well as during post entry. The distance education system being new, many people are not fully aware of the different dimensions of the system. The distance students are likely to carry with them to the system several wrong notions about the system prevalent in society. Hence, enough care is to be taken to provide proper information to the prospective students as well as students. Distance teaching institutions normally prepare and provide a variety of literature on the institution's goals, functions and processes. The British Open University has a number of such publications. An important source of information is generally the institution's newsletter. A newsletter can be an effective channel of communication between the University and its students.

Guidance Support

Guidance is a term with many meanings. It is a point of view, it is a group of services and it is a field of study. Guidance is a continuous process of helping the individual development to the maximum of his capacity in the direction most beneficial to himself and to society. Guidance involves help given by someone and is designed to assist a person to decide where he wants to go or how he can best accomplish his purpose. In the words of G.E. Smith, "the guidance process consists of a group of services to individuals to assist them in securing the knowledge and skills needed in making adequate choices, plans and interpretations essential to satisfactory adjustment in a variety of areas".

Studying at a distance facilitates personal development which often generates a need for guidance on how to fulfil new ideas and educational aspirations. Distance students, particularly joining lower level courses, need guidance on course choice. Undergraduate students in a distance teaching university have a wide freedom of choice within a modular system.

It might be argued that the demand for career guidance is less for the mature students. Since many have jobs already and look for career change or enhancement. The evidence proves otherwise.

Three quarters of the purely distance institutions around the world offer no career guidance at all.

Many dual mode institutions are providing career service to distance learners. Guidance is provided by a wide range of media: self directed materials, on-campus provision, telephone counselling, referral to local agencies, local advisors, outreach work, local workshops and use of present students and graduates as a resource.

The British Open University provides career guidance through a variety of means. Students receive guidance face to face, individually or in a group. Help is provided at a distance via printed materials, individual letters, telephone counselling or Computer Associated Vocational Guidance (CAVG). The printed materials include:

- Career planning
- Career choices and degree planning
- Undergraduate courses
- Recognition leaflets
- OU career booklets
- AGCAS graduate careers information booklets
- OU supplements to AGCAS Booklets

A senior counsellor in each region of the UKOU takes responsibility for the provision of local support and may advice students personally. All counsellors are expected to provide basic general advice on careers and course choice and to refer the student for specialist help where necessary.

A comprehensive system of career guidance should offer:

- Self analysis for the individual and what he or she is trying to achieve.
- Guidance on whether these aims are practicable and if so how to implement them.
- Information on careers and employment.
- Development of skills to deal with applications and interviews.
- Job placement: help in finding a suitable job.

Tutorial Support

Tutoring is a course related support provided by an individual for a particular learner or group of learners who also use prepared materials as a resource. It takes various forms but is mainly facilitating the learning of a known group of learners and is not replacing the materials. It is generally provided by a local tutor with whom learners are in direct contact. What tutors actually do varies widely, and they may have different titles in different systems - trainee, tutor counsellor, learning advisor, academic counsellor, teacher mentor, teacher tutor and so on.

A look at the range of activities of tutors collected from a number of distance education institutions goes some way towards describing both what he does and the need for him to do it. As Bernadette Robinson (1998) stated the tutor's function include some or more of the following activities:

- Commenting on students' written work,
- marking/assigning grades to students' written work,
- helping students understand course materials through discussion,

- answering student queries about the system,
- helping student plan their work,
- organising self-help groups or study circles,
- conducting face-to-face or telephone discussions,
- teaching at a residential school or personal contact programme,
- keeping records of students' progress,
- giving a lecture,
- giving a feedback on course materials and student problems to the local centre coordinator or counsellor or course writers,
- negotiating with the institution on the students' behalf when certain problems occur.

Tutorials (a) provide appropriate help towards mastering the academic content of the course units by providing explanation, clarification and reinforcement of the teaching materials, (b) offer opportunity for and assistance towards improving basic and course specific study skills appropriate to the level of study, (c) enable students to express, explore, modify, balance and test their knowledge and their ideas through group activities, (d) encourage and stimulate the students' academic progress, and (e) prepare students to become independent learners.

In Open Universities in India, an academic counsellor called by different names attached to study centres, performs the functions of a tutor and a counsellor while the Coordinator who heads a study centre shares the tasks of a counsellor. In the British Open University too at the foundation courses level tutor-counsellor performs the dual role, though at the Post-foundation courses level tutoring is separately provided by different course tutors.

The Manual for Academic Counsellors of IGNOU clearly suggested several important tasks for Academic Counsellors in relation to the students. The following is the checklist of tasks of the Academic Counsellors of IGNOU:

Helping towards mastering of units of courses:

- Explaining difficult concepts from Units
- Discussing problems
- arising in the counselling sessions
- anticipated by the counsellor
- Unlearning/discovering and correcting misconceptions

Improving study skills:

- Advising and giving examples of study methods

- Demonstrating skills and techniques
- Providing opportunities for individuals and group to practice
- Teaching students to use resources

Expanding knowledge through group activities:

- Providing opportunities for students to work with each other
- Generating discussion, suggesting activities, setting problem
- Encouraging contribution from all students
- Ensuring suitable layout and maintaining a relaxed atmosphere.

Encouraging academic progress:

- Relating students experience and previous knowledge to course material
- Advising on programme of study
- Helping students to keep to schedules
- Presenting the course as something interesting and enjoyable

Developing independence:

- Building up student self-confidence, motivation and moral
- Creating confidence in course material
- Encouraging self help activity

Early Attention on improving basic study skills:

- Note taking
- Essay writing
- Elementary mathematics
- How to learn from assignment comments

Counselling Support

Counselling is "the advice, help and support given to students to enable them to make satisfactory progress in the system". The kind of role a counsellor might play in a distance system is illustrated by the following list of duties for the British Open University Counsellors:

- advising applicants,
- providing induction meetings for new students,
- explaining the UKOU distance learning system,
- advising students on course choice,
- giving guidance on problems of an administrative nature, such as payment of course fees, choice of summer schools, withdrawal

from courses, late submission of written work, examinations, appeals,
- against tutor's grades, non-arrival of course materials,
- recording and monitoring of student progress and liaising with tutors,
- helping students to develop study skills,
- helping students to maintain motivation, and
- facilitating study-group activities.

Alan Tait (1987) mentions the main purposes of counselling:

- to give the student information on matters important to his success
- to get information about student which will be of help in solving his problems
- to establish a feeling of mutual understanding between student and teacher
- to help student work out a plan for solving his difficulties
- to help the student know himself better his interests, abilities, aptitudes, and opportunities
- to encourage and develop special abilities and right attitudes
- to inspire successful endeavour toward attainment
- to assist the student in planning for educational and vocational choices

Counselling is provided through different media in different distance education systems. The main media used for counselling are:

- Face to face counselling
- Group Counselling
- Telephone Counselling
- Counselling by letter
- Counselling by handbook
- Counselling by Audio and Video cassettes
- Counselling by Broadcasting
- Counselling by Computer

Library Support

There is an increasing recognition that student support services must include library services and library staff services. Library policies of different distance teaching universities in India and abroad vary from zero provision of books to elaborate library services. In India, there are more than 60 universities offering correspondence courses but their library services to external students are negligible. The library of the University of South Africa promotes distance teaching by providing elaborate library services. University of Manitoba in Canada, Universities of New England, Deakin University in Australia, and University of South Pacific in Fiji, offering regular as well as correspondence (distance education) courses, give high priority to the provision of library services to their on-campus as well as off-campus students. They have the same multi-tier system comprising central library and libraries at study centres as we have in the Indian Open Universities, but their library services are much more useful because they lend books through postal/courier services and some of them provide Xeroxed copies of journal articles from the central library, without any additional charges. In Thailand, students of Sukhothai Thammathirat Open University do not have access to libraries at their study centres. They usually use library services at the nearby public libraries, which keep the university study materials for general use by the public. The Public Library system in Thailand is well organised and has become very popular by promoting distance education and by providing library and information services to adult learners.

The Commonwealth of Learning has recently brought out a publication 'Library Services to Distance Learners in the Commonwealth'. The book provides readers with an opportunity to become acquainted with distance librarianship as it is practised in a number of countries in Commonwealth.

The library service needs of distance students can be divided into three categories:

- Materials and facilities;
- Information services; and
- User services.

The range of materials and facilities needed include:

- Reference books, text books and set books.
- Self instructional materials developed by various distance education institutions
- Audio visual material including computers needed to access information stored in various forms
- Typewriters, word processors, photocopiers and other types of reprography equipments
- Lecture halls and rooms for learners to meet and use audio visual materials;

- Library facilities for reading, storing and displaying materials to ensure quick and easy access to retrieve information.
- Self instructional materials, multimedia materials, educational programmes, radio broadcasts and television programmes on tapes, cassettes and discs.
- Distance education institutions courses and other information.

Other information that could be required is counselling programmes, summer and winter schools, laboratory and library facilities, special lectures, available resources and facilities.

Distance learners need professional assistance and support from the library staff on:

- Using the library collections
- Using reprography equipment and facilities available in the library,
- Providing guidance on the suitability of materials to support their courses, and
- Assistance in developing reading skills and study skills.

Canadian Library Association developed 'Guidelines for Library Support of Distance Learning in Canada'. Sometime back Australian government came out with Guidelines for Library Services to External students', Australia's Open Learning Agency has developed 'Open Learning electronic support services', American Library Association's college and Research Library's section brought out guidelines for extending library services. These documents are very useful for librarians of distance teaching institutions in providing different library and library staff services to distance learners.

Students as a Supporting Service

An important resource for student support is other students. The idea of peer group tutoring is a recent one. Students' organised groups can provide study group activities or supportive contact for isolated students. They are very useful for students in developing study skills and in overcoming particular problems in the texts. Structuring and organising student groups are facilitated by some distance teaching systems in the commencement of courses. As Bernadette Robinson puts it, student groups "are valuable in demonstrating to the students that not all knowledge resides in the person of the tutor, and they encourage students to take more responsibility for negotiating their own learning".

Regional Centres and Study Centres

In a distance teaching university, student support services are built on the concept of local centres. Local centres are normally of two kinds—regional centres and study centres.

The functions of Regional Centres in distance teaching universities include the following:

- Enquiry,
- Promotion,
- Student Admissions,
- Selection, Appointment and supervision of part-time Tutorial and Counselling staff,
- Training Tutors and Counsellors,
- Organisation of Special/Intensive/Mobile Tutoring and Counselling,
- Organisation of Weekend/Summer/Winter Schools, Residential Schools, Laboratory work, Field work etc.,
- Evaluation of Assignments of Students,
- Conduct of Examinations,
- Organisation of Annual Convocations,
- Promotion of Research on Distance Education,
- Setting up and maintenance of Study Centres,
- Periodical Meetings of coordinators and tutors, and Academic Counsellors, and
- Financial Administration of Study Centres.

A study centre is known by different names in different teaching institutions. Resource centres, access centres, outreach centres and learning centres are some of the terms by which study centres are known in different places. The most popular name is study centre.

The general characteristics of a study centre are:

- Shared space or reserved space in a local educational institution or non-educational organisation.
- Minimum equipment and facilities
- Local part-time staff
- Limited opening hours.

In most of the distance teaching institutions study centres are staffed by part-time staff. In some places full time staffs operate. The head and his/her supporting staff of a study centre have different names in different institutions.

Bradford, Kirk, Gough, Sewart, Northcott, Shapcot, etc. described how a study centre has been used for a number of functions in various distance teaching systems. "In some it has been seen as a viewing centre where replay devices may be used. In other it has been seen as library resources centre. In some it has been seen as a locus for student interaction and self-help groups, a substitute for the conventional campus. In yet others it has offered a site for practical experiments or the use of equipment, such as computing facilities, which are essential to study, but which cannot be offered to the student at home without great difficulty. Finally there are cases where study centres are seen as a tangible link between the otherwise amorphous distance teaching institutions and the local community".

The significance of a study centre can be well understood by the functions performed by it in open universities in Spain, Japan and Germany.

In Spain (UNED) Study Centres

- offer information and counselling for people who have not yet enrolled as students
- provide facilities for formal and informal student - student and student - tutor meeting
- acts as a cultural focus in the place it is located

In Japan (UA) Study Centres

- provide schooling, counselling, library resources, access to video audio cassette replay of broadcast lectures
- arrange proctored examinations for grading each subject at the end of the term
- provide a place for students to meet fellow students and faculty members

In West Germany (FU) Study Centres

- offer information and advice to registered students and enquiries on the degree programmes, entry requirement and other organisational and enrolment related details
- provide study material, literature and information brochures to browse through
- supply the necessary forms for registration, application, signing up for examinations, etc.
- Are supplied with technical equipment such as video and audio tape recorders and, in some instances, with computer terminals

or personal computers connected to the mainframe computer at the University's Central Offices in Hagen
- are the operating base for the mentors', as the part-time tutors help of the Fern Universtat are called
- offer help to students in the form of course-related seminars, individual or group tutorials, and preparation for assignments and examinations
- provide a venue for day or weekend seminars and for lectures by Fern Universitat professors and academic staff, as well as outside experts
- provide an opportunity for students to meet other students, either informally or in study groups

David Sewart (1981) writing on the significance of the study centres commented: "It is the richness and variety, multiplicity of provision, which attracts and sustains our students. Study Centres and what is offered in them are parts of this richness of provision… as part of the total package of the Open University teaching system, to which we ascribe overall the generic germ of teaching at a distance…. There is no contradiction between the students who do not attend the study centres, the Open University might come close to pure teaching at a distance. For others it will come less close…."

Student Support Charter

One way to improve the quality of service to students is to evolve a student charter by regional and study centres. The movement for such a charter has already begun.

In early 1990 Ormond Simpson (2002) wrote an Open University Student Charter for the UK Open University East Anglian Region. It specified standards of service in face to face and correspondence tuition, counselling and administrative services from teaching and counselling staff and Regional Centre. It also indicated how and who to contact at the Regional Centre. The motive behind the document was the feeling that too many students failed to progress because they were unable to ask for the help they needed. If such students know what services they want then they might feel better able to ask for those services and complain when they did not receive them. The draft charter was modified in the light of the objections and comments from colleagues and others. The term 'student charter' was given up and the document is now called "undergraduate and associate students services - your guide to teaching and counselling services is the UKOU East Anglian Region."

Ormond Simpson in his later presentation to the seminar on a student charter for Distance Education, at Laurentian University in Ontario, Canada reemphasised the usefulness of student charter. The seminar approved a number of elements as universal components for a student charter, which included

- providing clear information as to what was expected from students;
- publicising a procedure for dealing with student complaints;
- guaranteeing that the mode of delivery would not affect the award or credit;
- guaranteeing timely and effective feedback and commentary on assignments;
- guarantees re provision of library services where these are necessary;
- provision of academic counselling pre-study before selection of courses;
- access to tutor on a regular basis;
- the publication of clear information on administrative regulations;
- the right to complete a programme of study within agreed time scales; and
- the Charter should be related to the institution's mission statement.

14

Staff Development

Need for Staff Development

Staff development is one of the priority activities of a distance teaching system. In most of the countries a large number of personnel in distance education institutions are drawn from the conventional education system and hence training becomes imperative for equipping them with necessary knowledge, skills and aptitudes to perform the new tasks in new systems.

The need for training distance educators is well expressed by the UNESCO Regional Office for Education in Asia and Pacific in the following words: ".. the lack of trained personnel is a stumbling block. Most of the people, working in distance education have come from formal system and are attending to the methods of traditional education. Their new roles demand a new set of skills and attitudes, personnel must be reoriented and retrained for their changed task ....".

There are several theoretical and practical objectives of staff development. The Commonwealth of Learning (COL) Round Table Conference on Training (1990), emphasizing the importance of adequately trained manpower to improve the quality of distance education stated that training programme should:

- suit needs of the institution
- be available to all categories of staff
- suit the experience of the staff
- provide a sequence of training opportunities
- offer scope for career advancement
- employ a variety of strategies

Organization development greatly depends on the training of the staff of the organization. The role of training is greater in new type of organization.

'Staff development' is the new term for 'training' in distance education literature. Staff development refers to "the acquisition of knowledge and skills that people who work in distance education system need". As highlighted by Prasad (1994), the training of staff is an essential requirement of distance education system because

- distance education is a relatively new field and most of the staff who come from the formal system need orientation to distance education;
- training facilitates for the updating of existing knowledge and acquisition of new knowledge, new skills and positive attitudes are required for the job;
- training is a tool for staff development which refers to harmonising the individual and institutional goals;
- training results in more competence to do the job, resulting in more job satisfaction to staff;
- training builds up the capabilities for taking higher responsibilities thus paving the way for career advancement;
- training results in greater commitment on the part of the staff;
- training staff contribute to the better performance of the institution resulting in a better image, credibility and viability of the system;
- training is an effective mechanism to meet the needs and challenges of the information age;
- staff training is necessary for the adoption of new technologies;
- staff training provides a frame of reference for work;
- staff training provides opportunities for self-development and learning from experience;
- staff training is necessary to enable the institution to face the challenges of change;
- staff training provides trainees an over-all view of the system and helps them in relating their role to the system;
- staff training results in better services to the students; and
- the training of policy makers, educators and public men lends social support to the system.

The staff of a distance education institution generally includes:

- subject experts, usually the academics of the teaching institution,
- instructional designers,

- instructors to teach courses once they have been designed,
- specialists in leaner support,
- technology experts and technicians who set up and maintain the communications systems,
- administrators, such as programme directors, course managers and site
- coordinators,
- clerks who process enrolments, grades or materials, and
- managers such as deans, presidents and other executives.

Changing Roles of Distance Education Personnel

Practitioners/professionals at distance education institutions have roles fast changing such as

- A shift from teacher-centered to learner-centered forms of teaching/facilitation of learning.
- A shift in the "power base" between educator and learners, where the learners' needs determine the necessity of contact sessions and not the aims and objective of the lecturer.
- A shift from academic teaching roles for the transmission of knowledge to learners, to greater involvement in research, learning needs analysis, curriculum design and evaluation.
- The shift from the teacher as primary source of knowledge to the teacher a merely a resource person with some expertise in content.

Categories of Staff in Distance Systems

In higher distance education system several categories of staff perform varied tasks. Rumble (1986), a keen observer of the open university functioning, identified different categories of staff and their functions. All these categories of staff need training and retraining from time to time for effective and efficient performance of their tasks.

Tasks and Training Needs of Staff

A Regional Seminar organized by UNESCO Regional office for Education in Asia and Pacific attempted to identify different broad categories of personnel, their respective tasks and their training needs. Since the different categories of distance education personnel working in different countries are not exactly the same and do not operate or interact in one and the same manner, only broad categories of personnel, their tasks and

Staff Categories in Distance Education Systems

Function	*Categories of Staff*
GENERAL MANAGEMENT	Head of institution, departmental heads, and personal assistants and secretaries to these, planner with statisticians and other support staff, project control staff, institutional evaluators
Secretariat	Administrators (policy formulation and committee secretaries), secretaries/typists, filing clerks
Personnel	Personnel officers concerned with recruitment, training, industrial relations, terms and conditions of service, establishment control, secretaries and clerks
Management Services	Systems analysts, programmers, computer centre, managers, in-put clerks, etc.
Finance	Professional staff and supporting clerks concerned with accounts, staff payments, creditor payments, fees administration, financial planning, budgetary control, purchasing, some secretaries
Buildings and Estates	Buildings and estate planner, surveyor, services engineer, staff connected with utilities and services (plumbers, electricians, painters, carpenters), security guards, porters and internal mail staff, gardeners
Public Relations	Press and publicity officers, secretaries, house newspaper editor, etc
Catering	Kitchen staff, serving staff, etc.
Materials Development, Production & Presentation	Coordination by course or project leader, aided by project administrator, (and by scheduling and other professional staff as needed {e.g. Finance})
Library	Librarians
All materials	Curriculum planners, subject experts, educational technologists
Print	Editors, typists, word processor operatives, designers, graphic artists and photographers, copyright editors
Broadcasts & audio-visual	Producers, script-writers
Computer Assisted Learning	Programmers
Home Experiments	Technicians (to design equipment)
Tuition and Assessment	Senior tutors
Material Production	
Print	Editors, typesetters, printers

Function	*Categories of Staff*
Broadcasts/a-v	Designers, visual effects, model building and scenic construction staff, costume and make up staff, floor managers, studio assistants, camera crews, sound recordists, film and sound editors, announcers, presenters, actors, copyright editors, transport staff, etc.
Home Experiments	Production staff, assembly staff, technicians (to test equipment)
Computer Assisted Learning	Technicians
MATERIALS STORAGE AND DISTRIBUTION	Generally storemen, packers, and dispatch clerk
	For broadcasts on open and closed circuit transmission: appropriate staff concerned with their transmission
	For computer assisted instruction: operational and computer centre staff
Student Administration and Teaching Administration	Administrators, admission and student records clerks student enquiry service clerks
	Examination administrators, examinations and assignment clerks
	Tutor records office administrators and clerks
	Regional and/or local centre administration, secretaries and clerks, security guards, cleaners, etc
Teaching	Senior tutors and counsellors, tutors, demonstrators, counsellors, examination invigilators and script makers, etc.

training needs have been spelled out accordingly. Various personnel working in distance education are categorized by UNESCO Seminar under four heads as follows:

a) policy makers, planners, administrators and researchers;
b) personnel relating to the production of correspondence materials;
c) personnel relating to production of radio broadcasts; and
d) personnel relating to production of TV programmes.

The categories of personnel, their tasks and training needs identified by UNESCO Seminar are given here.

Tasks and Training Needs of Policy Makers, Planners Administrators and Researchers

Personnel	*Tasks*	*Training Needs*
1. Policy-maker and planner	1. Within the framework of national priorities, needs and constraints etc. conceives, plans and guides in the execution of distance education	1. Overview of distance education system, its strengths and weaknesses, its social need and economic viability 2. Knowledge of developmental plans in other sectors so as to relate education to the overall development of the country
2. Administrator	1. Overall manpower planning 2. Institutional Management 3. Co-ordination and supervision of institutional programmes 4. Popularising the distance education system 5. Some other specific tasks related to services in the field a under: a. Appoints tutors, allocates students to tutors. b. Deals with students and tutors problems c. Responsible for efficient tutor functioning d. Arranges staff and equips study centres 6. Schedules face to face sessions 7. Arranges other uses of study centres 8. Disseminates information to students 9. Supplies feedback to institutions 10. Collects marked assignments from tutors 11. Sends samples for monitoring 12. Conducts examinations, sends results to institutions 13. Regional publicity 14. Helps in admissions	1. Knowledge of Distance education and its operation at grass-roots level 2. Knowledge of institutions, programmes and procedures 3. Knowledge of distance education institutions working within the country as well as abroad and communicate with them. 4. Student and tutor problems 5. Training in Management and supervision of supporting staff. 6. Understanding of local conditions and problems 7. Skills in establishing rapport with community at grass roots level 8. Skills in human relationships
3. Researcher	1. Designs and carries out research in identified problems of distance education 2. Analyses and interprets data 3. Makes recommendations based on research findings 4. Compiles final report 5. Disseminates research	1. Understanding of distance education and its strengths and weaknesses and problem areas 2. Orientation towards various educational research designs 3. Sampling techniques with reference to distance education 4. Techniques of constructing instruments for data collection, analysis of data 5. Report writing 6. Dissemination skills

Tasks and Training Needs of Personnel Relating To Production of Learning Materials

Personnel	*Tasks*	*Training Needs*
1. Curriculum Designer	1. Assesses distance learners needs 2. Situational analysis 3. Conceptualizes and designs appropriate need based curriculum 4. Co-ordinates with others 5. Appreciates the role of media, face to face discussion and practical complements of the curriculum 6. Prepares course outlines 7. Suggests suitable learning experiences and activities 8. Helps in the preparation of learning outcomes 9. Helps in evaluation of curriculum	1. Overview of distance education system its strengths and weaknesses etc. 2. Understand of needs, resources, constraints etc. of distance education in general and those of the institution in particular 3. Knowledge of target groups and their problems 4. Knowledge of learning experiences and activities, etc. 5. Knowledge of teaching strategies 6. Curriculum designing skills 7. Understanding the role of media in distance education 8. Evaluation of curriculum skills
2. Writer/ Reviewer	1. Decides/adopts format 2. Organizes material 3. Develops detailed educational strategies 4. Writes correspondence lessons, usually in close collaboration with other members of course team 5. Supplies ideas/drafts for illustrations 6. Revises drafts 7. Works with reviewers, editors and illustrators until material is ready 8. Tests, and evaluates material 9. Revises/reviews galley proofs from printers 10. Prepares feedback questionnaires pretests and post-tests	1. Overview of distance education system, its strengths and weaknesses, etc. 2. Knowledge of writing/reviewing skills 3. Knowledge of target groups and their problems 4. Knowledge of learning process and teaching strategy 5. Knowledge of content 6. Locating resources/materials etc. 7. Knowledge of production of materials through course team 8. Testing and evaluation skills 9. Some knowledge of design editing and printing possesses.
3. Editor	1. Face-editing: format, student-aids layout, print get-up 2. In-depth text editing 3. Collaborates with authors to remove content ambiguities and confusions 4. Language editing 5. Checks readability, logical flow, sequencing and presentation of material 6. Checks suitability of illustrations, graph making, etc 7. Proof-reading 8. Contacts printers to get the material printed	1. Overview of distance education system, its strengths and weaknesses 2. Knowledge of distance teaching techniques 3. Editing skills 4. Presentation, layout skills 5. Marking-up manuscript for printing 6. Proof-reading skills 7. Knowledge of different media and their role in teaching 8. Knowledge of printing stages

Personnel	*Tasks*	*Training Needs*
4. Course Coordinator	1. Schedules and arranges course development, maintenance and renewal activities 2. Briefs external writers 3. Coordinates activities of course team 4. Facilitates services to ensure smooth course production 5. Collaborates with course team members 6. Prepares student and tutor guides and other supplementary materials such as assignments, tests, marking guides etc, for mailing 7. Arranges review and testing of materials 8. Communicates with students and tutors from time to time 9. Monitors tutors marking of assignments 10. Arranges workshops/practical components, if necessary	1. Orientation in philosophy of distance education 2. Writing skills 3. Coordination skills 4. Sound knowledge of subject content and methodology 5. Course production procedures 6. Scheduling, communication 7. Management skills 8. Testing and evaluation
5. Tutor/ Evaluator	1. Corresponds with students 2. Holds face to face sessions 3. Gives prompt, accurate and constructive feedback to students on their progress 4. Marks assignments 5. Sends in results 6. Provides guidance and counselling to students 7. Provides feedback on students problems and procedural difficulties	1. Know about distance education and its various aspects and tutors role in it 2. Role of evaluator in distance education 3. Knowledge of the subject content 4. Knowledge of programmes, schedules, regional services, facilities 5. Skills in communicating with students 6. Counselling skills 7. Human relationing

Skills Required by Staff

In the preceding sections, various categories of personnel are identified. Consequently, their task specifications and training needs were also spelled out. They give a synoptic view of various skills required by various personnel. These tables are helpful in delineating various skills which should constitute the content of the training programmes designed for that category of personnel.

In the preceding section, an attempt is made to identify training skills for various personnel. As there are many personnel needing different skills, it is well highly impossible to draw up specific training programmes for

Personnel in Educational Radio and their Tasks and Training Needs

Personnel	*Tasks*	*Training Needs*
1. Script Writer	1. Writes scripts in different formats with certain criteria of radio programmes for educational purposes.	1. Knowledge about distance education and its various aspects 2. Theory and practice of radio script writing 3. Basic training in programme production
2. Producer	1. Helps assist and collaborate with the script writer in the development of script 2. Evaluates a radio script 3. Uses equipment for radio/audio recording 4. Select suitable music and sound effects 5. Selects suitable casts/presenters 6. Leads a recording team 7. Edits radio programmes	1. Criteria of good radio programmes 2. Principles of Script Writing 3. Radio recording instruments 4. Music and sound effects 5. Radio casting 6. Radio production 7. Programme editing
3. Programme Evaluator	1. Evaluates the impact of the programmes 2. Writes research reports research	1. Knowledge about distance education and its various aspects 2. Programme evaluation and audience 3. Research Report Writing
4. Utilizer	1. Utilises the programmes effectively	1. Knowledge about distance education and its various aspects 2. Listening in groups 3. Listening individually 4. Pre-activities of listening 5. Post-activities of listening 6. Feedback mechanism

each category. However, training programmes can be envisaged at two levels: one to provide general information about distance education and the second to provide specific skill competencies for different jobs. The general course can be called the "*Foundations and Skills*" course and the job specifics, '*Options*'. The foundation course may take between 25 and 35 hours and options between 50 to 60 hours. The foundation and options courses can also be designed at two levels, one for personnel working in distance education institutions and other for field workers.

Strategies for Staff Development

Most strategies used for staff development in the conventional systems of education are used for distance education systems also. The following are the popular strategies used for staff development.

Personnel in Educational Television and their Tasks and Training Needs

Personnel	Tasks	Training Needs
1. Producer	1. Develops production-ready scripts 2. Selects proper techniques of presentation keeping in view the requirement of the original text 3. Selects proper compare and the talents for the programme 4. Guides the production staff such as set designers, cameraman, sound effects man, special effects man and the engineers	1. Knowledge about distance education and its various aspects 2. Theory and practice of TV production with special emphasis on the following a) Selection of proper sets b) Camera movements (shooting process) c) Appropriate formats and techniques in production d) Programme editing
2. Script Writer	1. Writes scripts based on curriculum to interpret, explain and elaborate certain portions in the texts 2. Determines the right format for a script	1. Knowledge about distance education and its various aspects 2. Theory and practice of TV script writing 3. Formats it TV script writing 4. Basic knowledge about TV production
3. Designer **- Graphics** **- Illustrations** **- Set designing**	1. Develops visuals, sets, illustrations and other material keeping in view the requirements of scripts 2. Understands and carrys out the instructions of the producer and provides him with sets and other visual material for production	1. Knowledge about distance education and its various aspects 2. Training on ETV set designing 3. Training in graphics 4. Training in developing visual materials for education
4. Special Effects man (visual)	1. Provides the producer with the required visual special effects to enhance the impact of the programme 2. Develops and conceives appropriate visual special effects for educational TV	1. Knowledge about distance education and its various aspects 2. Training in (visual) special effects.
5. Sound effects man	1. Provides the producer with the required sound effects 2. Training in audio special effects	1. Knowledge about distance education and its various aspects
6. Utilizer	1. Utilizes the programme with skill to derive maximum benefit out of it	1. Knowledge about distance education and its various aspects 2. Viewing programme in groups 3. Viewing programmes individually 4. Pre-programme activities 5. Post-programme activities 6. Feedback mechanism
7. Programme Evaluator	1. Evaluates the programme 2. Writes research report	1. Knowledge about distance education and its various aspects 2. Programme evaluation and audience research 3. Research Report-writing.

- Workshops
- Field Staff Programmes
- Manuals
- Professional Associations
- In-Home Programmes
- Assistance from Resource Institutions
- Consultancy
- Attachments
- Visits
- Adoptions

Pre-Service Face to Face and Distance Education/Training Programmes on Distance Education

Some distance higher education institutes (single mode and dual mode) are offering education programmes with discipline of distance education. These Programmes serve the purposes pre-service training programmes, some of which are:

- Diploma in Distance Education (from Associates of European Correspondence Schools)
- Diploma in Distance Education for External Students (from International Extension College, UK.)
- Diploma in Distance Education (From Sri Lanka OU).
- Graduate Certificate in Distance Education (From University of New England, Australia).
- Graduate Diploma of Distance Education (for Deakin University, Australia).
- Master of Distance Education (from Athabasca University, UK Open University, Maryland University, Southern Queensland University)
- Postgraduate Diploma in Distance Education & Master of Distance Education (From Indira Gandhi National Open University, India).

More of the above programmes are designed to provide the skills, understanding and professional knowledge appropriate for staff involved in developing and maintaining distance education programmes at all levels of schooling and post-secondary education. More particularly, the programmes of studies focus on the characteristics, theory and practice of distance education for people whose primary responsibility lies in the preparation of learning material, the provision of technical services, teaching and counselling support for students, and the administration and management of distance education programmes. The concepts of distance education developed in the courses cover all those forms of organised education in which the goal of learning is not achieved by regular face-to-face teaching".

Causes of Failure of Staff Development

Robinson (1998) suggests that the causes of failure in staff development are:

- Opposition or apathy in senior staff
- Simply serving those few individuals who volunteer
- Ignoring and avoiding hard-core resistance.
- Inadequate resourcing.
- Inappropriate content, strategies, time tabling and devotion.
- Training being too theoretical, didactic or remote from the realities of the workplace
- off the organizational culture
- Time-lag between training and implementation.
- Lack of follow-up.

These factors need to be taken into account in planning staff development programmes.

Evaluating Staff Development

There is no automatic guarantee that any staff development strategy will succeed. Robinson (1998) suggest that evaluating staff development involves considering the contexts, process and outcomes and asking the following questions:

Context

- How accurately were the strategies diagnosed? What data were used and how they were analyzed?
- Why was this particular training mode/strategy adopted?
- How were the objectives determined? What were the objectives? What kind of outcomes did they focus on? Was the training event appropriate to these needs/objective?
- How does this staff development initiative link to the experience of the participants?
- How does it link to their other training? How does it link to the overall staff development plan?

Process

- What resources were available (human, financial, physical, time). Which of these were actually used? Were these appropriate?
- Was the selection of the participants appropriate?
- What was the participation rate
- Were these problems of workload, demands placed upon or time-release for the participants?
- Were the designs, organization and implantation of the staff development appropriate? What is the evidence for this?
- Was this the best or most appropriate way of providing this aspect of professional developments?

Outcomes

- How many participants were involved?
- What was the short term impact of the training event on the participants?
- What was the long-term impact?
- Was the training efficient?
- Was it effective?
- Was it cost-effective?
- What remaining or new needs were identified?
- What follow-up or other further action needed?

15

Technologies for Distance Education

Communication is central to education. For over 3,000 years, from Homer, Moses and Socrates onwards, the teacher, in direct, personal contact with the learner, has been the main means of educational communicating knowledge. When the invention of thc printing press facilitated, for the first time, the large scale spread of knowledge through books. Printed materials however did not replace the teacher. Teachers retained their role in educational process.

The introduction of postal service helped the introduction of correspondence education. Postal service was followed by telephone. Then came the radio. It is interesting to recall that the first Director of Education at the BBC thought about the possibility of a "broadcast university". The first adult education talk by BBC was on 6th October 1924. The first schools radio programme was broadcasted by the BBC in 1926. Sixteen mm film came into use from the 1930s, to be later replaced by, to a great, extent by television. School television began in 1957 on a regular scale. Bates (2005) records the introduction of divergent new technologies into teaching upto 1980 and from 1980 as follows:

Upto 1980: Types of Technologies

- Teacher
- Printed Book
- Postal Service
- Telephone
- Radio
- Film
- Television

From 1980: Types of Technologies

- Audio cassettes
- Audio-conferencing
- Audio-graphic systems
- Video cassettes
- View data/Teletext/Teledom
- Computer based learning
- Laser video discs
- Cable TV
- Satellite TV
- Expert systems
- LCD Projectors
- Search engines
- Mobile Phones
- Wireless networks
- Compact discs
- E-portfolios
- Video cassettes
- Video conferencing
- Electronic mail
- Computer conference
- Internet
- World Wide Web
- Digital video discs
- Fiber optics
- Learning objects
- Portals
- Simulations
- Virtual reality

Media and Technology

Media and technology can be distinguished. The term media describes a generic form of communication associated with particular ways of representing knowledge. Each medium not only has its own unique way of presenting knowledge, but also of organising it.

In education, the 5 most important media are:

- Direct Human contact (face-to-face)
- Text (including still graphics)
- Audio

- Video
- Digital multi-media (incorporating text, audio and video)

While certain technologies are closely associated with each medium, a variety of different technologies may be used to deliver these media.

Generations of Distance Education

There have been many significant and worthwhile attempts by scholars to explain the developmental cycles of distance education. While all of them have viewed Distance Education (DE) developments from pedagogic, managerial, technological, and other perspectives, the most widely used classification from the technological point of view is that of Taylor (2001), who identified five global generations of distance education technology:

1. Correspondence model
2. Multimedia model
3. Tele learning model
4. Flexible learning model
5. Intelligent flexible learning model

Taylor (2001) has provided a comparative analysis of these models based on flexibility (with regard to time, place, and pace), learning materials and interactive delivery.

Models of Delivery

In addition to defining the generations of distance education: there have been numerous interpretations of the ways distance education is delivered. This of course, depends on the institutional vision and mission; the philosophical/ideological stance on the nature of client groups and the curricular provisions; the state of technological preparedness, geographical coverage, and the institutional strategic niche, among other factors. Otto Peters (2001) describes eight models which are indicated below:

1. Examination preparation model
2. Correspondence education model
3. Group distance education model
4. Learner centered model
5. Multiple mass media model
6. Network based distance education model
7. Technologically extended classroom teaching model
8. Virtual university model

Generations of Distance Education and Delivery Technologies (Taylor)

Models of Distance Education and Associated Delivery Technologies	*Characteristics of Delivery Technologies*			
	Flexibility			*Advanced Interactive*
	Time	*Place*	*Pace*	*Delivery*
First Generation – The Correspondence Model				
• Print	Yes	Yes	Yes	No
Second Generation – The Multimedia Model				
• Print	Yes	Yes	Yes	No
• Audio tape	Yes	Yes	Yes	No
• Videotape	Yes	Yes	Yes	No
• Computer-based learning (e.g. CML/CAL)	Yes	Yes	Yes	Yes
• Interactive Video (disk and tape)	Yes	Yes	Yes	Yes
Third Generation – The Telelearning Model				
• Audio teleconferencing	No	No	No	Yes
• Videoconferencing	No	No	No	Yes
• Audio graphic Communication	No	No	No	Yes
• Broadcast TV/Radio + Audio teleconferencing	No	No	No	Yes
Fourth Generation – The Flexible Learning Model				
• Interactive multimedia (IMM) online	Yes	Yes	Yes	Yes
• Internet-based access to www resources	Yes	Yes	Yes	Yes
• Computer mediated communication (CMC)	Yes	Yes	Yes	Yes
Fifth Generation – The Intelligent Flexible Learning Model				
• Interactive multimedia (IMM) online	Yes	Yes	Yes	Yes
• Internet-based access to www resources	Yes	Yes	Yes	Yes
• Computer mediated communication, using automated response system	Yes	Yes	Yes	Yes
• Computer portal access to institutional process and resources	Yes	Yes	Yes	Yes

Distance Teaching Institutions use Variety of Technology

Distance teaching institutions use a variety of communication technology. The British Open University's charter specifically enjoins it to advance and disseminate learning and knowledge "by teaching and research by a diversity of means such as broadcasting and technological device appropriate to higher education". One of the objectives of Indira Gandhi National Open University is "to advance and disseminate learning and knowledge by a diversity of means including the use of any communication technology…". In fact, some of the open universities have titles signifying the influence and importance of communications technology. The prominent examples are: Japan's University of Air and China's Radio and Television Universities. Thus a notable feature of distance learning system is "the planned use of a wide range of media…suited to the needs of the students". The British Open University was originally conceived as the "University of Air".

Technologies used by distance education system are categorized into four by Robin Mason (1999).

1. Text-based systems, including e-mail, computer conferencing, real time chat systems, fax and many uses of the web.
2. Audio-based systems such as audio conferencing and audiographics and audio on the web.
3. Video-based systems such as videoconferencing, one way and two way; video on the Internet with products like CU S See Me, Web-casting and other visual media such as video clips on the web.
4. Web which integrates text, audio and video, both as pre-prepared clips and as live interactive systems, both real time and stored to be accessed later as well as access to educational resources of unprecedented magnitude.

The detailed description of these technologies is given by A.W. Bates in his landmark work *Technology, E-Learning and Distance Education (2005)* and by Michael Moore and Greg Kearsley (2005) in their stimulating work *Distance Education: A Systems View.* Some technologies are described here.

Audio and Video Technologies

Important audio and video technologies include

Audio Technologies	*Video Technologies*
Radio	Television
Audio Cassettes	Video cassettes
Audio graphics	Video discs
Audio conference	Computer disc
Audio vision	Video text
Telephone	Teleconference

Radio

The potential advantages of radio for use in learning at a distance programme included "time, cost-effectiveness and localness". While not always essential to most programmes, radio is particularly useful in complementing printed information. Radio can accelerate or extend learning at distance programmes and is useful in reaching isolated rural audiences quickly and relatively inexpensively. While radio programmes are restricted by broadcast time schedules, they are an important component of learning at a distance programmes at the elementary, secondary and post-secondary levels in both industrialized and developing countries.

It was not until the late 1800s that radio became a reality. Ilertz proved the existence of radio waves in the 1880s; less than twenty years later, Marconi transmitted wireless signals across the Atlantic. The invention of the triode vacuum tube amplifier became the "magic lamp" of radio, and with the AC plug-in, radios became a widespread household convenience during the 1920s. After the transistor was invented in 1948, radio became even more widespread. It is now a highly cost-effective way of broadcasting information throughout the entire world.

Today, radio can be used (and often is used) to enrich the material delivered to students who are learning at a distance. The popularity, availability, and low cost of radio make it a convenient and practical medium for use in programmes for learning at a distance. Furthermore, the use of radio can overcome problems associated with illiteracy. However, programmes provided by broadcast radio do have one serious limitation: listeners must be available at the scheduled broadcast hours.

The U.K. Open University listed down the following uses of radio.

- To provide remedial tutorials or some other forms of tutorial based on feedback.
- To provide corrections, alterations or updating of material, where print re-make budgets are limited, or where print cannot reach students quickly enough.
- To bring to students primary resource material, i.e., recordings which, through careful editing and selection, can demonstrate principles covered in the units. This material may be used in a number of ways.
- To bring to students the views and knowledge of eminent people, which can be condensed in an interview, or be edited afterwards, to provide the essential points, which may be more complex or lengthy in written form.

- To record especially the voices of people who have not been recorded before, but whose contribution to the course would provide a unique experience (e.g. famous poets reading their own work, civil servants talking – perhaps anonymously – about their role in decision making).
- To change student attitudes
- To bring alive the performing arts direct into the student's own home, and to demonstrate methods or techniques of drama or music through performances.
- To provide the student with a condensed argument, in lecture form.
- To enable students to perceive the different points of view that exist, and observe ideas being challenged, through discussion and interviews.

In practice, radio never became an integrated and essential component in more than a few courses – mainly in the Arts faculty. Even in the early years, when the transmission times used were still convenient for large numbers of students, the average listening rate was not much over 50 percent; that is, each radio programme was heard, on the average, by little over half of the students for whom it was intended. And as early as 1974 it was reported that on the majority of OU courses, radio programmes were somewhat peripheral appendices to the printed material.

Television

While radio is generally acceptable, television is not. The case against the use of television for education is based on the following reason:

- Television is no doubt a technologically brilliant medium but it is a format for entertainment, not for education as it is inherently hostile to thought.
- It is in the nature of the medium to trivialize everything it touches and to free the viewer from the obligation to think.
- All ideas are reduced to a lowest common denominator. Television image is one of "low definition" and offers little detail.
- Television suppresses the content of ideas in order to accommodate the requirements or visual intent, i.e. to accommodate the values of show business.
- Television is a low involvement medium; students will be required to do nothing more than watch and television viewing produces an alpha brainwave pattern state (relaxed, inattentive condition).

- Television is synonymous with entertainment and commercials; it is difficult to treat it for serious business.
- Educationists may have brilliant ideas of teaching but they have to accommodate them to television and not *vice versa*.

The advocates of television for education give the following reasons;

- Electronic communication is a fundamental change on a par with previous great revolutions such as writing, printing and the telephone and will result in the most far-reaching changes in social progress.
- Many educationists have realized that a piecemeal approach to television results in the waste of a most powerful educational tool. If well used, television is as effective as a good teacher and if badly used is as ineffective as a bad teacher. "At least, both educational institutions and the community in general are beginning to awake to the fact that television is not just a trivial and passing phenomenon suitable only for entertainment, but is a medium which could be as significant for education as is print itself. Furthermore, the converging technologies of televisions and computing promise even more exciting developments in the future."
- Educational methods must make use of the fact that we remember what we see, more than what we hear – which is one of the most distinguishing features of television.
- The remarks on brainwaves and low involvement are not based on tested generalizations.
- Nor is it correct to make television the scapegoat for any upsurge of violence in a society. The link between television and violence has not been scientifically established.
- Television in fact humanizes distance education. The human face on the screen established a rapport and the mass medium in this way really delivers the message on an individual basis.
- Television generates a sense of belonging among the participants of distant education as it enables the sharing of the same programme with thousands of others similarly motivated.
- Most of the criticism of television is in the context of the social situation in the US which need not necessarily happen elsewhere. Not in all countries, for example, do children spend more hours before a television than in school.
- For the educationalist, the debate is really not 'either-or', in other

words, the question is not whether television should be used or not as the sole purveyor or lessons; the question is how far television can be used with other media. Television cannot solve all problems.

- It is in the hands of the educationist to ensure that the format does not become more important than the context. Television can in fact take over some of the routine tasks and allow more time for profitable interaction with students when tutors meet them.

The UKOU listed down the following uses of Television:

- To demonstrate experiments or experimental situations, particularly:
- To bring to students primary resource material, i.e. film or video recordings of actual situations which, through editing and selection, can demonstrate principles covered in the units. This material may be used for a number of purposes, for example
- To record special events, experiments, species, places, people, buildings, etc. which are crucial to the content of units, but may be likely to disappear, die or be destroyed in the near future.
- To bring to students the views or knowledge of eminent people, who are often prepared to be televised but not to write material especially for the institution.
- To change student attitudes:
  - To explain or demonstrate activities that the students are to carry out (e.g. home experiments, survey interviewing).
  - To provide feedback to students 'mass' or total result of activities or surveys carried out by the students themselves, where the turnaround time is too short for printed feedback.
  - To illustrate abstract principles involving dynamic change or movements.
  - To illustrate abstract principles involving thorough use of especially constructed physical models.
  - To illustrate principles involving two, three or n-dimensional space.
  - To use animated, slow-motion, or speeded-up film or videotape to demonstrate changes over time (including computer animation).
  - Through performance, to demonstrate methods or techniques of dramatic production, or different interpretations of dramatic works.

- To demonstrate decision-making processes.
- To condense or synthesize into a coherent whole a wide range of information which, in print, would take up considerable space and would not provide the richness of background material necessary for students to appreciate fully the situation.
- To demonstrate how basic principles have been applied in the real world, where visualization of the application in its total environment is necessary to understand the way the principle has been applied, and the difficulties encountered.
- To test students' ability, by requiring them to apply concepts or principles learned elsewhere in the course; by explaining or analyzing real-life situations presented through television.
- To demonstrate the use of tools or equipment, or the efforts of tools or equipment.
- To demonstrate methods of playing instruments, and the relationship between music, musicians and their instruments.
- To increase students' sense of belonging; identification of and with course designers; to make the teaching less impersonal.
- To reduce the time required by students to master content.
- To pace students; to keep them working regularly; to break the inertia in beginning evening study.
- To recruit or attract new students (either to the University or to specific courses); to interest general viewers in subject matters.
- To establish academic credibility of the course to outside world.

Video-Audio Cassettes

Video Cassettes are a comparatively recent educational media. It is a child of broadcast television. The features of video cassettes and broadcast television are same. Unlike television, video cassettes can be played independent of predetermined transmission times. The main educational advantages of television programmes are involvement, dramatic impact, dynamic properties and rich symbol content. These advantages apply equally to cassette recordings of broadcast television programmes or to video cassettes made ab initio for using as cassettes. Video cassettes provide students full control of the medium over television broadcast. The student can watch the programme whenever he wants and as often as he likes.

In recent years the British Open University provided a video cassette loan service for students of select courses in response to deterioration in the transmission in times available for Open University television broadcasts.

Students gave these main reasons for borrowing cassettes:

> (1) access, (2) control, and (3) level. They took advantage of the flexibility of cassettes to study the programmes at times convenient to them and in phase with their own study patterns. They could view the programmes as often as they liked. They were able to adjust to pace of the programmes to suit their own needs as necessary.

In the British Open University, the greatest media development in the recent times has been the audio cassettes. The University is now making more material for use on cassettes than on radio. Audio cassettes are becoming very popular. Academics like them as they can exercise control over their use and can integrate them more tightly into course design. The use of the channels – sound and vision – in a controlled and integrated way, through the combined use of cassette and print or media, is a very powerful teaching medium. They are ranked as the most useful component next to correspondence texts. In some courses they have been ranked as the most useful component of the course. They are liked by students because of their convenience and informality. Students frequently feel that cassettes are as good as having as personal tutorials with the course author in their rooms. Audio cassettes allow for mastery learning, explanation and discussion of graphical, tabular and printed conceptual material, practice in problem solving and exercise in mathematical processes.

Telephones

Telephone is a potential powerful educational tool. Recent years have seen a rapid growth in the use of telephone as an educational media. Teaching by telephone has been used in a number of distance education contexts and in a variety of ways with individuals and with small and large groups.

Telephone offers two way interactive communication across distance. The means of providing telephone link may be terrestrial wire or cable, high frequency radio waves, micro-waves or satellite. Although most familiar in its domestic form, telephone also has other capabilities. By means of a telephone network, audio, video and data information can be sent and received by individuals or large groups of people.

Teaching by telephone covers a variety of usage. They refer to:

- courses and students taught wholly or largely by means of an instructional telephone conferencing network with minimal accompanying printed material;
- courses taught on campus but 'attended' by distant students via a telephone link;
- courses taught partly by correspondence materials, partly by group teleconferences;
- courses taught mainly through correspondence material (perhaps with other media as well, such as television, radio or audio cassette) and which offer supplementary tutorial support by means of telephone (either individual or group);
- courses where telephone communication is an integral part of the teaching event, for
- example, a live television or one-way video presentation followed by students telephoned questions, which are both asked and answered on air;
- individual telephone calls (occasional or regular) to course writers or tutors from remote students with particular problems in understanding printed course materials;
- individual telephone calls to tutors from remote students needing advice or counselling in relation to educational problems

In a British Open University study telephone tutorials are found to be used effectively for the following tasks;

- to clarify student difficulties in course materials;
- to promote student discussion of specific issues and topics;
- to exchange interpretations of a case or thesis;
- to discuss problems of recent written assignments, or strategies for tackling forthcoming ones;
- to check through worked answers to previously-circulated problems;
- to analyse a written text or a musical score;
- to present short case-studies
- to debate a prepared case for or against a thesis;
- to role-play an exercise;
- to practice and evaluate sight singing on a music course;
- to identify and clarify concepts in genetics using previously circulated worksheets;

- to manipulate symbolic expressions, using previously circulated diagrammatic material;
- to construct and evaluate graphs, using previously circulated worksheets;
- to interpret and discuss previously circulated sets of raw data;
- to negotiate the design of a project in cognitive psychology and monitor its progress

Computers

Computers have been used extensively in education for more than twenty years, yet they have had little impact on distance education. Ehin wrote about this more than ten years ago and remarked on the absence of literature dealing specifically with computer applications in correspondence education. However, recent advances have led to increased capabilities at substantially lower costs. Two developments can be identified as most important. The first is the development and mass distribution of microcomputers; the second is the marriage of computers with communications technology, making direct and inexpensive computer communication both possible and relatively inexpensive. Computers can be used in distance education systems in two modes, referred to as local mode and transmitted mode. Local mode is synonymous with 'off line' since the computer stands alone as an independent system. Peripheral devices such as disc drives or printers are often used to enhance the system. In transmitted mode, a computer or terminal is connected to another computer ('on line') and the operation depends upon communication between these devices. By the inter connection of computers, it is relatively simple to create a complex learning network which could theoretically link all distance learners with their teachers and with a central institution. An electronic university could be created as described by Turoff and established by a private enterprise firm in San Francisco. Other examples include word processing to aid course development, and data processing to aid administration and student registration.

The instructional process in distance education is divided clearly into two stages. The first stage involves the design, development, physical production and storage of instructional materials. Cooper and Thompson have discussed text processing as a powerful tool for authors and editors. Its use in creating and editing documents facilitates the development of manuscripts before the production stage. Editorial changes, additions and deletions no longer delay development or add major costs. By also providing a course writer and a course designer each with microcomputer, communications software, and a modem to connect to the telephone lines, the development process can be even more significantly enhanced. With this addition, all of the text processing options are still available, but electronic mail can be used to communicate changes and exchange materials. If a course team approach is used with multiple writers and other professionals, this approach can be extended by using computer conferencing. By adding computerized page-composing, computer graphics, and computerized photo-typesetting, the production process could also be automated, where the manuscripts (with inserted graphics) could simply be left on a data base for electronic access by learners. At the present time, text processing is used by most institutions dedicated to distance teaching or having major distance education departments. Some institutions such as the Open Learning Institute and Athabasca University also use computerized photo-typesetting systems. The course material is then stored in a warehouse using a computerized inventory control system to maintain and route material.

The second stage of the instructional process involves delivery of the material to learners. Significant contributions to this area will begin to occur when distance learners have their own personal computers (or computer terminals), although limited benefits are possible if access to centre is provided.

Although text processing is a useful tool for student use in their assignments, the real breakthroughs here will occur through the use of computers to provide direct instruction. Computer-aided learning (CAL) has already been used at the Open University in Britain to provide diagnostic feedback, remedial help and revision aids.

It appears that many courses would benefit from the use of CAL modules. The ability of a computer to simulate real-life situations which are not available to learners due to high cost, danger of other factors, is a resource which should be brought to the distance learner. Examples are courses requiring laboratory work (such as chemistry), practical work (such as process control), decision making (such as business or economics). Baath and Phillips and Young both presented evidence to show that the use of CAL increased completion rates in distance education courses. Many learners have or can be provided with access to suitable microcomputers for at least limited periods. This would permit the inclusion of shorter CAL modules where appropriate.

Another area which promises to increase the efficiency and effectiveness of distance education is computer-managed learning. TV Ontario has already begun to make use of this method to a limited extent.

In the continuing education courses, learners throughout Ontario return their assignments on computer marked sheets. The computer-managed learning software marks the assignments and automatically generates personalized letters with results and appropriate feedback. These letters are then mailed to the students using the mailing labels also generated by the computer.

The major innovation in this whole area is computerized communications. This includes electronic mail and computerized conferencing, which permit one-to-one and one-to-many communications among many people using computers and communication lines. An additional powerful feature is the ability to search and retrieve information from large-scale computerized databases, opening up the possibility of remote libraries such as already available with the abstracts on the ERIC system. Computer conferencing as understood here is the use of computers to link people together across time and space. Cross has observed that 'computer teleconferencing is a system which enables two or more individuals at two or more locations to communicate'. Without having to interrupt their work schedules and to pay for costly travel, these individuals can exchange information and learning aids. Through keyboards, terminals, printers and telephone lines, participants access a common computer for extremely efficient direct communication.

Herasim and Johnson have outlined several general features of computer conferencing systems. These include text editing, sophisticated searching capabilities for conference items, access to external databases, and electronic messaging. In addition, computer conferencing systems usually maintain a permanent record of proceeding during the course of a conference, thus serving as a type of electronic filing cabinet.

The final area where the computer has been extremely useful and will continue to be so may be termed 'instructional support'. For example, the Open Learning University has been using computers in most of its internal operations. Examples include a computerized student registration system, tutor records, course development, an inventory system in the warehouse, library research database, and internal communications.

Web-based Learning

The big breakthrough for online learning came with the development of the world wide web and the consequent rapid spread of the Internet into many homes, offices and higher education institutions in more economically advanced countries. The first web-based university courses started appearing in 1995.

The University of British Columbia in Canada, offered its first credit courses delivered entirely over the Internet to distance education students in 1996. At the same time, Murray Goldberg, a young computer science professor at the University of British Columbia, developed software package called 'WebCT' specifically designed to enable web-based courses to be offered over the Internet.

There are several important educational features that distinguish asynchronous computer mediated communication from other technologies. First, is that the learner can be in regular touch with teachers and other learners even though they are not physically present. Second, communication is not synchronous, but forwarded, stored any accessed at the learner's convenience. Third, a vast array of digital resources can be accessed through electronic networks and downloaded into the learner's or teacher's own computer and stored for later use.

From 1996 onwards, the classroom teachers started to incorporate the Internet into their regular classroom teaching. Hybrid, blended or mixed mode are all terms used for integrating the Internet into regular classroom teaching. This is still the most prevalent form of online learning. There are several ways to supplement classroom teaching.

Most distance education programmes began their use of Internet by adding online elements to existing print and broadcast based materials, such as e-mail communication between teacher and students, submission of assignments as e-mail attachments and online discussion forums.

Web-based learning provides several kinds of interaction: (a) interaction with learning materials, (b) interaction between students and teacher, and (c) student-student interaction.

According to Bates (2005), web-based learning can be cost competitive with print based form of distance education, and much more cost-effective than broadcasting technologies, for moderate numbers of students per course. Web-based learning does not have the same economies of scale found with either print or broadcasting. Rather than economies of scale, web-based learning offers the potential of economies of scope.

It is possible to offer individualized courses more cost-effectively to small numbers of distance learners. Online courses can be tailored more easily to the needs of individual students. Web-based learning offers the opportunity to achieve academic goals such as creative and critical thinking, knowledge construction, problem solving and collaborative learning.

Given that the web was not applied earlier until 1995, as Bates commented, it may be too early to decide whether an actual paradigm shift is occurring in education due to the development of the Internet and the Web…there is a long way to go before web-based learning becomes a pedagogical paradigm shift…

Selection of Technology

Bates suggests a model for technology selection and application which have the following characteristics:

- It will work in a wide variety of contexts;
- It allows decisions to be taken at both a strategic, or institution-wide, level, and at a tactical, or instructional level;
- It gives equal attention to instructional and operational issues;

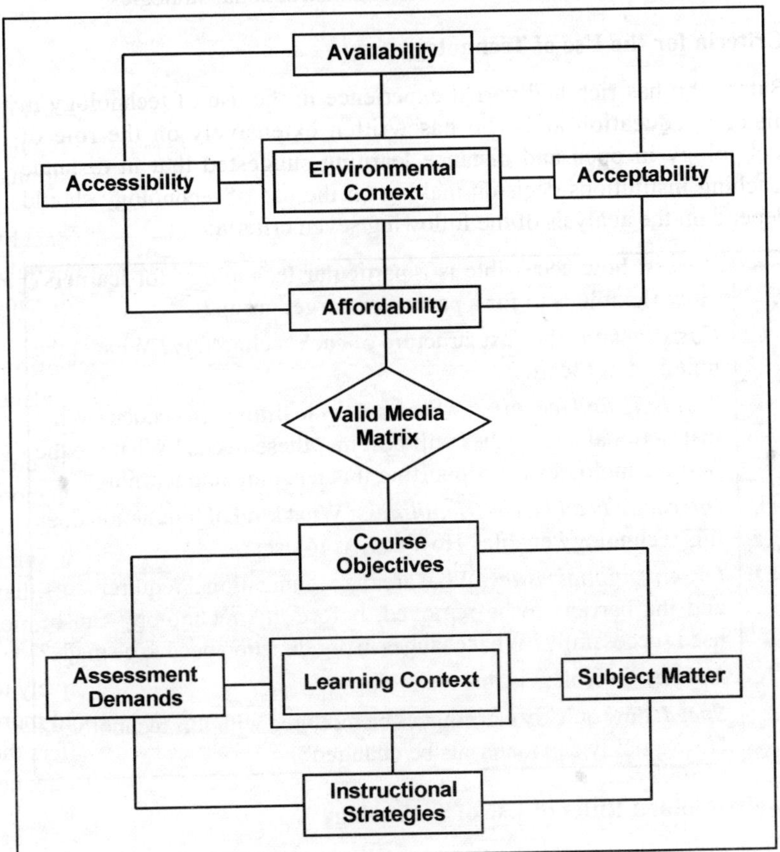

Selection of Valid Mix of Technologies

- It will identify critical differences between different technologies, thus enabling an appropriate mix of technologies to be chosen for any given context;
- It will accommodate new development in technology.

Selection of Valid Media Mix

The selection of valid media mix would depend upon two kinds of contexts, i.e. environmental and learning. As environmental context is concerned, media must be chosen in the light of four criteria such as availability, accessibility, acceptability and economics. As learning context is concerned, media must be appropriate to four criteria such as course objectives, assessment demands, subject matters and instructional strategies.

Criteria for the Use of Technology

Bates who has rich and varied experience in the use of technology in distance education and who has written extensively on the role of technology in open and distance learning suggested that in distance teaching institutions decision making on the use of technology should depend on the analysis of the following seven criteria:

A	*Access*: how accessible is a particular technology for learners? How flexible is to for a particular garget group?
C	*Costs*: what is the cost structure of each technology? What is the unit cost per learner?
T	*Teaching and learning*: what kinds of learning are needed? What instructional approaches will best met these needs? What are the best technologies for supporting this teaching and learning?
I	*Interactivity and user-friendliness*: What kind of interaction does this technology enable? How easy is to user?
O	*Organizational issues*: What are the organizational requirements, and the barriers to be removed, before this technology can be used successfully? What changes in organization need to be made?
N	*Novelty*: how new is this technology?
S	*Speed*: how quickly can courses be mounted with this technology? How quickly can materials be changed?

Twelve Golden Rules of Use of Technology

Bates (2005) proposed twelve golden rules of using technology in education and training that apply whatever technologies are being used:

1. *Good teaching matters*: Clear objectives, good structuring of learning materials and relevance to learners' needs, all apply to the use of any technology for teaching. If these principles are ignored, then the teaching will fail, even if the unique features of the medium are exploited. Good teaching may overcome a poor choice in the use of technology, but technology will never save bad teaching.
2. *Good design is essential*: Proper instructional design is essential for proper courses.
3. *Each medium has its own aesthetic*: Each medium and technology has a different range of production skills necessary to export its unique features.
4. *Education technologies are flexible:* Technologies are flexible and hence interchangeable in education and training. The absence of a particular technology does not necessarily present learning from being achieved.
5. *There is no super technology*: All technologies have their strengths and weakness. They therefore need to be combined.
6. *Make all five media available:* Ensure that face-to-face, print, audio, video and digital multimedia is available for teaching purpose in one form or the other.
7. *Interaction is essential:* High quality interaction with learning materials, interaction between teachers and learners and interaction among learners are all essential for effective learning.
8. *Student numbers are critical:* The total number of learners to be served over the life of a course is a critical factor in technology selection.
9. *New Technologies are not necessarily better than old ones:* There is no law that says new technologies will automatically be better for teaching than old ones.
10. *Teamwork is essential:* No one can know everything there is to know about the educational use and design of every technology now available.
11. *Teachers need training to use technology effectively:* Teachers and instructors need training not only in the choice and use of technologies, but also in how people learn and how to teach with technology.
12. *Technology is not the issues:* The issue is: how and what do I want students learn. There is more than enough technology around now to allow you to teach in whatever way you choose.

16

Quality Assurance in Distance Education

Quality assurance in open distance education today is entrenched widely in national and institutional policies and practices. The jargon of quality assurance has entered the lexicon of the common practitioner of open distance education, and even resource poor institutions have set up some mechanisms of assuring quality, however rudimentary.

The quality assurance of open distance education is a frequent topic of discussion in many international gatherings and remains a challenge. Does the quality assurance of distance education require processes that are different from those used for quality assurance in traditional setting? Is the quality assurance of open educational resources a separate issue again? Can the quality of rapidly evolving open education resources and e-learning materials be assessed at all?

The distance education guidelines of the Quality Assurance Agency for Higher education, UK, argue that distance education quality needs to be assured in the same way as any other form of higher education.

To establish credibility and equivalence, quality assurance in open distance education must address the following organizational differences:

- Large number of stakeholders, specialists or sites involved in development and delivery.
- Separation of learners and institution.
- More separate activities, roles and participants.
- More detailed planning of production and budgets in advance of programme presentation.
- More administration tasks distributed between different sites and partners.

- More diverse target audience.
- Greater use of the web and other ICTs.
- More delegation of aspects of learning and assessment to local or workplace partners.
- Distributed organizational structure for material creation, teaching or learner support.
- Different interpretation of what constitutes teaching, for example, a learner based instead of a lecture based approach.

Quality in open distance education is frequently judged in term of learning materials because of student learning is all the centre of the open distance education experience. Success depends on how effectively course production, delivery and student support sub-systems operate, underpinned by academic standards and management processes.

Organizing and managing quality in open distance education is essentially about managing operational and academic standards, which means establishing those standards and ensuring their regular review.

Quality Assurance Considerations

Important quality assurance considerations for open distance education are:

- Curriculum and instruction
- Staff support
- Student support
- Student outcomes

Student outcomes are very significant consideration which means:

- Establishing acceptable rates of student progression and retention.
- Developing mechanisms for monitoring student progress and strategies for identifying and responding to problems.
- Ensuring that the students can progress by examining scheduling, calendars mode of offering and pre-requisites.
- Developing strategies to monitor standards of performance within subjects and across courses and programmes, identifying external standards.
- Developing distributing and monitoring policies on assignments submission, grading practices and grade distribution.

officials and the public of the accredited status of an institution as a reliable indicator of quality.

- An expression of confidence in policies and procedures of the institution by its peers - a lasting source of pride.
- An external source of stimulation to improve services, programmes and staff, through periodic evaluations by an outside independent group of peers.
- Assurance of high standards of educational quality through the adherence to established criteria, policies and standards.

The benefits of accreditation of higher educational institutions by Indian National Assessment and Accreditation Council (NAAC) include:

- Helps the institution to know its strengths; weaknesses and opportunities through an informed review process.
- Identifies internal areas of planning and resource allocation, enhances collegiality on the campus.
- Provides funding agencies objective data for performance funding.
- Initiates institutions into 'innovative and modern methods of pedagogy.
- Gives institutions a new sense of direction and identity.
- Provides society with reliable information on quality of education offered.
- Provides access to employers on the quality of education offered to potential recruiters.
- Promotes intra and inter institutional interactions.

India's Distance Education Council recently set up National Accreditation Committee for Open and Distance Learning (NACODL) to accreditate institutions offering distance education courses on the lines of conventional universities accredited by NAAC. Infrastructure and human resources, relevance of programmes, student support system, employment opportunities, research, consultancy and governance will be assessed by NACODL. Some recent changes occurred in the system of Accreditation.

Quality as a Culture

Koul (2006) looked at quality assurance, in the context of quality as culture, along three dimensions: (1) the core dimension, (2) the systematic dimension, and (3) the resource dimension.

The core dimension pertains to learner centric and capacity building. The systematic dimension pertains to the initiation and introduction of quality assurance mechanism, internal as well as external, the symbiotic relationships between the two and the management of both the mechanisms and the relationships. The resource dimension pertains to the pivotal factors that make changes possible and durable.

A quality culture is an institutional culture that promotes the introduction of an internal quality assurance system, values the capacity building for implementing quality assurance arrangements, stresses the link between the internal quality assurance system and accountability to the public at the national and international levels and focuses on learning rather than learning quality culture has been merging, if not fully integrated. All major distance teaching universities have developed and implemented quality assurance standards and procedures in key areas of distance education activities.

It is found that international organization such as UNESCO, COL, OECD and World Bank have provided useful quality assurance guidelines and recourses for distance educators.

Quality assurance in distance education researches beyond local and regional boundaries and new forms of distance education provisions are increasing. Distance education in a globalised context requires new quality assurance mechanisms because the existing ones do not address the challenges of recent distance education markets. There have been internal debates, guidelines, corrections and best practices developed. The key to successful quality assurance activities in the future lies in distance education institutions' commitment to internal debates and international decision making process related to quality assurance issues.

country rather than Distance Education accreditation. However, institutional accreditation standards must consider Distance Education's nature, system and different modes of academic delivery, including mixed mode delivery. Distance Education specialists should be involved in setting the minimum accreditation standards and in serving on peer review panels for universities offering Distance Education components.

For example, the Open and Distance Learning Quality Council in the United Kingdom offers institutional accreditation to all its providers of home study, distance learning, online learning and other open learning or flexible learning courses that meet their standards.

In India the National Assessment and Accreditation Council (NAAC) offers voluntary accreditation. Accreditation rests on seven criteria applied to all institutions: curriculum, teaching, learning and evaluation, research, consultation and extension, infra structure and learning resources, student support and progression, organization and management are healthy practices.

In 2009, the Distance Education Council (DEC) in India setup the National Accreditation Committee for Open and Distance Learning (NACODL) to accreditate institutions offering education through distance mode. The Distance Institutional Accreditation by DEC will comprise the following framework:

- Programme design and development
- Programme transaction and delivery
- Student assessment and evaluation
- Research, consultancy and community engagement
- Learner support services and progression
- Infrastructure and learning resources
- Government structures and leadership
- Internal quality assurance process
- Innovative practices

In 2014, Distance Education Bureau of UGC took the functions of DEC.

As the world of distance education expands and changes the need to ensure that courses and programmes offered through distance education meet minimum standards of quality has become more important than ever. Although the recent past has seen much controversy, debate and uncertainty, it appears that the accreditation community has begun to adopt in large and small ways – the accreditation practices and standards applied to traditional institutions and programmes, and apply them to distance education institutions and programmes.

18

Leadership in Distance Education

Leadership in distance education is focused less in the literature on distance education. There is a wide gap in the research literature on distance education leadership.

Beaudoin (2003) reviewed the literature which was published in the I990s, by conducting a content analysis of: (I) the titles and abstracts that appeared in the *American journal of Distance Education*, and *DEOSNEWS*, an electronic journal, both published by the American Center for the Study of Distance Education; (2) 1998 and 1999 issues of *Open Learning*; and (3) 1997-1999 issues of *Distance Education*, and found only a few articles related to distance education leadership. He concluded that "over a four-year period, several widely read sources of research and writing in distance education theory and practice offer us very little indeed on the topic of leadership". Beaudoin also conducted content analysis of presentations at: (I) the European Distance Education Network, Bologna, Italy (1998); (2) the Distance Education Conference, sponsored by the University of South Africa (2000); and (3) the ICDE World Conference on Open Learning and Distance education, held in Dusseldorf, Germany (200I), and found that "the interest and attention focused on the general theme of distance education management, in general, and leadership, in particular, was conspicuously thin"

The books devoted to open and distance education leadership and management are not many and included those of Dunning, Vankekrik and Zabrowski (1993); Freeman (1997); Paul (1990); Cynthia (1998); Latchem and Hanna (2001) and Beaudoin (2005).

Emerging leaders in distance education will need to be well versed in the business functions of their universities and colleges so that system and structures operate smoothly and effectively for students, faculty and

- lack of a sense of humour
- Insincerity – trust is fundamental to the success of a leader and it can quickly be undermined by any of the following – giving different messages to different groups, participating in catty gossip, or being openly manipulative in almost all dealings with people.
- Insecurity – it is almost impossible to convey a sense of direction and confidence if one is displaying personal insecurities.

Emerging Distance Education Leaders

Emerging distance education leaders can be responsible for part or all of the dimensions and factors involving a distance learning initiative. Depending on the scope and functions of a specific programme, a leader may need outside resources to maintain consistency. Simonson, Smaldino and Zvacek (2009) discuss Anthony Kaye's four subsystems of a distance education system that include all the regulatory subsystem, course subsystem, student subsystem and logistical subsystem. Within each of these categories exists a multitude of administrative and leadership functions. The authors outline a distance leader pyramid of competencies that include and have been listed topdown as visioning, leading, managing, designing and knowing. Within these constructs, an emerging distance teacher must be knowledgeable in various areas such as policy, regulation, state and federal government influences, financial aid, copyright, data gathering, regional, national and professional accreditation, accessibility, intellectual property rights, faculty issues and finally, the costs and budgetary influences associated with distance learning agenda.

Leadership is a set of attitudes and behaviours that create conditions for innovative changes, enable individuals and organizations to share a vision and more in the appropriate direction and contribute to the management and operationlisation of ideas.

Emerging leaders in distance education not only must be transformational leaders but must also became situation leaders who are innovative visionaries that can motivate, energize, inspire, and induce others to more forward while fully articulating a shared and competitive distance learning agenda. Beaudoin (2002) states that emerging leaders in distance education need a variety of skills that are constantly refined and those include resource mobilization, needs assessment, fitting technology to needs, programme evaluation and accreditation, policy formulation strategic planning, operationalising ideas, market analysis, implementing online infrastructure, collaborating with partners, training and support for faculty and mentoring the next generation of leaders. Simonson (2004) commenting on the distance learning leaders said:

> A distance learning leader is a visionary capable of action who guides an organization's future, it vision, mission, goals, and objectives. The leader guides the organization and its people who have faith in the leader and have a clear understanding and acceptance of the organization's worthwhile and shared vision and goals. A distance learning leader has competence in knowing, designing, managing, leading and visioning distance education.

example, by bringing an increased awareness of health care as a result of a particular course or series of courses, or by increasing awareness of the educational needs of adults.

- *Generation of knowledge*: the extent to which distance education contributes knowledge useful to a better understanding of the learning process.

Four Point Criteria of Keegan and Rumble

Keegan and Rumble (1982) appraised the successes or failure of nine DTUs over the decade 1971-80 using a four-point assessment scheme—(1) the quality of the learning achieved, (2) the quantity of learning achieved, (3) the status of the learning achieved and (4) the relative cost of the learning achieved. They did not deal with internal efficiency. Keegan (1996) recommended the four point evaluation for the overall evaluation of any distance teaching system.

The sub-criteria under each of the four main criteria used by Keegan and Rumble (1982) are as follows:

i) The quantity of the learning achieved under these headings are considered:
   - the success of the system in widening access, not just in terms of absolute numbers, but in attracting specific target groups;
   - drop-outs;
   - the quantity of the output relative to the input (the output/input ratio);
   - the time it takes to produce the output; and
   - the system's success in satisfying national local and individual needs.

To receive a satisfactory evaluation the institution is required to achieve measurable success in: (i) the avoidance of avoidable drop-out; (ii) the number of successful students as a proportion of the number of students admitted; and (iii) the time it takes for students to achieve successful outcomes.

ii) The quality of learning achieved

Under this heading are considered:

- the quality of the learning materials provided by the distance system;
- the extent to which distance teaching is a suitable vehicle for educating students in certain subjects;

- the extent to which education is provided as opposed to instruction;
- the effectiveness of learning at a distance; and
- the 'inter subjectivity' of learning at a distance.

iii) The status of the learning achieved.
Under this heading the following are considered:

- the extent to which other educational institutions recognize the studies for credit transfer purposes;
- the acceptance of the degrees and diplomas awarded as qualifying students to go on to higher level studies;
- the recognition of the awards by employers; and
- the esteem in which the distance teaching in institutions and their awards are held in the community at large.

The status of distance programmes can be measured and data collected for evaluation on the extent to which other educational institutions recognize the studies for credit transfer; the acceptance of the distance degrees for higher level studies; and the recognition of the awards by managers in competitive interviews for employment.

iv) The relative cost of the learning achieved under this are considered:

- the cost efficiency of distance universities relative to conventional universities or to other modes of internal operation which the distance universities could adopt;
- the cost effectiveness of distance universities relative to conventional universities - the concept of cost effectiveness tries to weigh the relative value of the outputs in qualitative terms;
- the cost benefits of distance and traditional university education, in which the costs of the education provided and the benefits (direct and indirect, financial and social) to the individual and society are taken into account; and
- the opportunity cost of education at a distance.

Other Criteria

There are other criteria by which activities and programmes of Distance Teaching Intuitions could be evaluated. McIntosh, Kemmis, and Rumble are prominent among those who provided different criteria of assessment of effectiveness of distance education.

McIntosh emphasizes formative evaluation, defined as evaluation that is conducted in conjunction with the development of a new educational programme with the aim of influencing that develops.

Kemmis suggests four levels of evaluation. (1) programme evaluation, concerning general institutional relationships, (2) curriculum evaluation, concerning the educational arrangements of curricula and particular courses, (3) evaluation of student, concerning the opportunities for learning created by a particular teaching learning encounter, and, (4) students assessments concerning the outcomes of student learning.

Rumble basing on Gooler's criteria but taking into account various criteria suggested by others provides an evaluative analysis of distance education institutions on the seven criteria— (1) access, (2) relevancy to needs and expectations, (3) quality of programmes offered, (4) learner outcomes, (5) effectiveness and efficiency, (6) impact and (7) generation of knowledge.

Performance Indicators

In recent years considerable interest is developing in the development of performance indicators as an aid to educational management and as a means of assessing the overall performance of an institution. Many now feel that there should be a series of performance indicators that can be used in non profit making service organizations like distance teaching universities to measure the effective and efficient accomplishment of the expectations of the institution's constituencies. Sorenson and Grove who worked on 'Cost-outcome and Cost-effectiveness Analysis: Emerging Non Profit Performance, Evaluations Techniques' indicated several service performance indicators. Of these the significant ones are availability, awareness, acceptability, accessibility, appropriateness extensiveness, effectiveness and outcomes benefits/impacts. Rumble (1986) ably summarized each of these service performance indicators by applying to distance education.

The development of performance indicators has its roots in the dissatisfaction of the U.K. government, in the early eighties, regarding the effectiveness of its universities. This was first manifested in the form of a green paper (Department of Education and Science, 1985) on the Development of Higher Education into the 1990s which pressed for improved contribution from the educational sector in national economic development. It demanded that higher education should be more responsive to the requirements of the economy, should try to obtain increased private funding and should not be heavily dependent on public funds, should display greater selectivity in the allocation of research funding, and should be more cost conscious managing its resources efficiently and effectively. A Steering Committee, set up by the Committee of Vice Chancellors and Principals, to examine the efficiency and effectiveness of universities, in its report (the Jarratt Report) recommended that reliable and consistent performance indicators needed to be developed. It suggested that "a range of performance indicators should be developed covering both inputs and outputs and designed for use both within individual institutions and for making comparisons within institutions".

Performance Indicators as Applied to Distance Education

Availability	Increased earning power of ex-students/graduates, benefits to society, local community, other educational institutions, etc.
Awareness	Knowledge of DE system among user population (courses offered etc.)
Accessibility	Hours of opening of local study centers, broadcast transmission hours, access media in the home
Extensiveness	Student enrolments against target numbers/quotas, number of users of special services, percentage use of media
Appropriateness	Demand for courses/Service; mismatch between demand and availability
Efficiency	Cost per service per student per course, etc.
Effectiveness	Comparison of planned to actual; Percentage utilizing facility or service; graduate success in employment etc. budgeted to actual cost; planned to actual cost per student course; planned to actual wastage rates
Acceptability	Demand for courses, number of complaints about course content or services, complaints about speed for service
Outcomes/ Benefits/ Impacts	Increased earning power of ex-students/graduates, benefits to society, local community, other educational institutions, etc.

Taking into consideration various criteria suggested by different distance educators and writers, a set of criteria appropriate to current conditions to evaluate the performance distance higher education system with particular reference to open Universities is evolved by some modern distance educators. The suggested criteria include:

- Relevancy to needs and expectations of people
- Availability of courses
- Extensiveness
- Quality of courses offered
- Effectiveness and efficiency
- Learner outcomes
- Access
- Impact
- Generation of knowledge.

20

Distance Education Research

In 1950s scholarship in distance education began through systematic research in the United States, the leaders being Gayle Childs and Charles Wedemeyer. Childs in 1949 wrote one of the first doctoral thesis on correspondence education and initiated one of the first studies on educational television. Childs conducted a national study sponsored by the University Extensions Association on enrolments in correspondence course, in 32 colleges and 24 high schools. Mackenzie, Christensent and Rigby in 1968 published a study on correspondence instruction in the United States with the title *Correspondence Instruction the United States: A Study of What it is, How it is, How it Functions and What its potential may be.*

Two volumes of *the Brandenburg Memorial Essays on Correspondence Instruction* by Wedemeyer during 1963-66 proved to be great works. As commented by Moore, of monumental importance in the history of distance education, Wedemeyer's ideas were incorporated into the design of the revolutionary new Open University of the United Kingdom, the first publicly funded, national autonomous degree granting distance teaching university.

In Europe during 1960s, two distance educators, i.e., Borje Holmberg and Otto Peters enriched scholarly writing on correspondence education. Holmberg's *On the Methods of Teaching Correspondence (1960)* initiated the first European awareness on pedagogy of correspondence studies.

Otto Peter's while working at German Institute of Distance Education Research at the University of Tubingen, undertook an inventory of correspondence/distance education in more than 30 countries and developed his theory of industrialized education.

Holmberg (1986, 1989, 1995) argued that distance education research established itself as a scientific discipline, which can be described both in terms of a recognized basis of theory, its research programmes and in terms of a curriculum for University study. Holmberg noted that in 1982, there were fifteen recognized fields of research within the sphere of distance education. His 1982 categorization of research fields and academic programmes identified the following subjects:

- A general analysis of distance education, its philosophy and theory.
- Undergraduates and graduate studies, as well as student motivation
- Curriculum design and study goals
- Curriculum development
- Media
- Chronologically spaced, not continuous, interactive communicational tutorials
- Lifelong lessons
- Counselling
- Design, organisation and administration of educational institutions
- Economics of distance education
- Evaluation
- History of distance education
- Distance education in the developing world
- Guidance for distance education teachers
- Research into research

It is fascinating to view the fields of research into distance education as they stood in 1982 in the light of the correct situation and the host of new factors that have emerged and enriched the field.

Over the years a number of reviews of distance education literature have been published in which the authors developed categorization schemes of research areas:

- Scriven (1991) used the following nine headings to classify articles that were published in the first ten years of the journal *Distance Education*: (1) students and their characteristics; (2) specific programmes and courses; (3) telecommunications and media; (4) specific countries-practices and procedures; (5) theory; (6) course design and development; (7) economics and management; (8) counselling and student support; and (9) tutors, staff development, staff involvement.
- A similar study was conducted by Koble and Bunker (1997) for The American Journal of Distance Education (1987-1995) with

the following classification: (1) theory, policy, and development; (2) media and delivery systems (effectiveness, evaluation, methods); (3) institution, staff, and management; (4) student psychology, motivation, and characteristics; (5) faculty participation and instructional process; (6) course design and curriculum development; and (7) student administration and support.

- In the same year, Mishra (1997) published an analysis of periodical literature in distance education (1991-1996) with seven major groups and 34 sub-groups of research topics. The major groups in this classification are as follows: (1) distance education in perspective (including open learning, growth and development, equity and access); (2) students and their learning (including learner characteristics, drop out, cognition, student support, interaction, and feedback); (3) learning materials and related issues (including design and development of study materials, learning from media); (4) technology issues; (5) management issues (including planning, economics, evaluation, and quality assurance); (6) distance education theory, research and training/professional development; and (7) distance education in practice (including distance education institutions and teacher education).
- Rourke and Szabo (2002) applied nine categories for a content analysis of the *Canadian Journal of Distance Education* (1986-2001): (1) administration: budgeting, change, inter-institutional cooperation, staffing; (2) evaluation: judgment of the worth, value, success of a course, programme, or courseware; (3) foundations: semantics, definitions, history, models; (4) instructional design: course, programme, or product design, development, and delivery; (5) instructor characteristics: satisfaction, motivation, attitude, perceptions, teaching style, gender, demographics; (6) international perspectives: practices, procedures, role of distance education in specific countries; (7) learner characteristics: satisfaction, motivation, attitude, perceptions, learning styles, cognitive styles, attrition, gender, demographics; (8) technology and media: educational radio, educational TV, video, audio, computer conferencing; and (9) trends: discussion of the general direction or inclination of issues and topics in the field.
- Lee, Driscoll, and Nelson (2004) developed a system consisting

of six categories for grouping distance' education literature: (1) design-related topics: needs, assessment, course scheduling, course design, instructional strategy development, course material design, and visual design; (2) development-related topics: course support system and material development, web-based learning management system building, online tools development, and online testing system development; (3) management-related topics: learning resource management, troubleshooting, attrition rate, faculty and staff support, learner support, and technical support; (4) evaluation-related topics: programme quality control, assessment of learning outcomes, benefits and cost analysis, return on investment, evaluation of supporting system; (5) institutional and operational-related topics: administration, academic affairs, accreditation, certification, policy, payment, and budgeting; and (6) theory and research-related topics: distance education theory building, review of literature, introduction to new research methods, culture and gender issues, learning style, history of distance education, and copyright law.

Regarding methods in distance education research, several researchers follow several methods. Naidu (2004) suggested five methods: (i) case studies, (ii) correlation studies, (iii) experimental studies, (iv) phenomenological studies (v) development research; and (vi) research synthesis.

Berge and Mrozowski (2001) indicated four methods: (i) descriptive methods, (ii) case study, (iii) correlation research and (iv) experimental research. Lee (2004) classified into seven areas: (i) theoretical inquiry, (ii) experimental research; (iii) case study; (iv) evaluation research; (v) development research; (vi) survey research and (vii) combination inquiries.

Bermord (2004) discussed methodological issues with a view to improve the qualitative reserve in distance education. These include (i) lack of experimental control, (ii) lack of procedures for randomly selecting research participants, (iii) lack of random assignments of participants to treatment conditions, (iv) poorly designed dependent measures that lack reliability and validity, and (v) failure to account for a variety of variables related to the attitudes of students and instructors or a failure to at least properly report essential information about these aspects of study design.

Jegade, OJ (1994) highlighted the difficulties faced by experts in the commonwealth countries with understanding research in distance education. The following are the difficulties:

- Time allocation
- Funding
- Lack of personal interest in research projects
- Finding a researchable problem
- Access to relevant literature
- Lack of institution's interest in research effort
- Professional advice
- Finding right audience
- Competency in research methodology
- Lack of personal enhancement from research.
- Report writing
- Research project management

COL's Policy on Research

The objectives of COL's research policy are to:

- sustain the leadership role of COL as a specialist organisation in the application of ODL to development;
- maintain its competitive edge as a provider of policy advice and know-how to Governments, intergovernmental bodies and institutions;
- strengthen its role by investing proactively in research relevant to the development and growth of ODL;
- stay ahead of developments in ODL in order to respond to the needs of member states at various stages of development in their use of ODL;
- contribute to the professional development of COL staff; and
- sustain a culture of research appropriate to a learning organisation

COL confines its research initiatives to areas related to its corporate mission and programmes. This includes topics such as the following:

- ODL in development—education, health, governance, food security, business etc.;
- Organisation and management of ODL systems;
- Perspective planning—methods and practices;
- Design and development of instructional systems;
- Materials development—organisation, methods and practices;

- ICT in open learning and distance education;
- Technology choices: factors, forms and functions;
- Learner Support systems: organisation and management;
- Student evaluation systems and procedures;
- Costs, costing systems and financing;
- Institutional evaluation and performance assessment;
- Quality, relevance and access;
- Cross-border provision of ODL;
- Potential areas for COL's intervention in different contexts: national, regional and global;
- Partnerships and cooperation at regional and international levels.

Separate Centres for Promotion of Research

Distance teaching institutions developed research policies and set up separate centres, units or departments at their institutions. For instance, the UKOU established the Institute of Education Technology with substantial research capacity. It has become a leading institute in research on distance education. Some of such other Institutions are:

- International Research Foundation for Open Learning, UK
- American Centre for the Study at Distance Education, USA
- Canadian Institute of Distance Education Research at Centre for Distance Education, Athabasca University, Canada
- Centre for Research in Distance and Adult Learning, Open University of Hong Kong
- Institute of Distance Education, Korea National Open University, Korea
- Staff Training and Research Institute of Distance Education, Indira Gandhi National Open University, India
- Centre for Research in Distance Education, Central Von Ossietzky University of Oldenburg, Germany.
- Distance Education Centre, University of Southern Queensland, Australia
- Centre for Flexible and Distance Learning University of Auckland, New Zealand
- South African Institute for Distance Education, South Asia
- Research Centre, Sukhothai Thammirat Open University, Thailand
- Central Institute for Distance Education Research, Fern Universitat, Germany

Research on distance education has been subject to harm and consistent critique (Berge and Mrozowski, 2001; Bernard *et al.*, 2004; Saba, 2000). Moore (1985) stated that there is "a massive volume of amateur, unsystematic and badly designed research questions are rarely posed within a theoretical framework or based on its fundamental concepts and constructs" Perraton (2000) feels, "an examination of research shows that it is often a theoretical and predominantly descriptive"

Subjects for Research

Howell, Williams and Lindsay (2003) identified 32 trends in the distance education literature. According to them, any of these could be the subject of a doctoral or other research study.

1. Student Enrolment Trends

- Distance education programmes are necessary because current higher education infrastructure cannot support the demand
- Students are shopping for flexible courses
- Higher education learner profiles are changing
- Adult, female and minority learners are increasing
- Retentions is of concern to administrators and faculty

2. Faculty Trends

- Traditional faculty roles are shifting or unbundling
- Need for faculty development, support and training is growing
- Faculty tenure is being challenged, allowing for more non traditional faculty roles in distance education.
- Some faculty members are resisting technological courses delivery
- Instructors of distance courses can feel isolated.
- Faculty members demand reduced workload and increased compensation

3. Academic Trends

- Knowledge and information are growing exponentially
- Institutional landscape of higher education is changing: traditional campuses are declining, for-profit institutions are growing and public and private institutions are merging.
- There is a shift in organizational structure towards decentralization
- Instruction is becoming more learner-centred, nonlinear and self-directed.

- Growing emphasis on academic accountability.
- Academic emphasis is shifting from course-completion to competency.
- Education is becoming more seamless between high school, college and further studies
- Higher education outsourcing and partnerships are increasing
- Some advocate standardising content in learning objects.

4. Technology Trends

- Technology devices are becoming more vertical and ubiquitous
- Huge growth of internet usage
- Technological fluency is becoming a graduation requirement

5. Economic Trends

- With the economy in recession, there are fewer resources for higher education and higher education initiatives, such as distance education
- Funding challenges are the top IT concern for many
- Lifelong learning is becoming a competitive necessity

6. Distance Education Trends

- More courses, degrees and universities are becoming available through distance education programmes. The internet is becoming dominant among other distance education media
- Distinction between distance and local education is disappearing
- The need for effective course management system and web services is growing.
- There is an increasing need for learning and teaching strategies that exploit the capabilities of technology.

21

Some Developments and Trends

1. Globalisation of Distance Education

Globalisation is a process through which an increasingly free flow of ideas, people, goods, services and capital would lead to the integration of economies and societies. It is characterized by an accelerated flow of trade, capital and information, as well as mobility of individuals, across geographical borders. It reflects comprehensive level of interaction than that has occurred in the past. It implies a diminishing importance of national borders and strengthening of identities that stretch beyond those rooted in a limited locale in terms of particular country or region.

The global distance education system offers courses directly to students using distance education technologies across a number of countries, possibly on regional basis or on a multi-regional basis. It does this in a conscious and planned way.

The development of modern Information and Communication Technologies (ICTs) has greatly helped the emergence of global distance education systems. New institutions claiming to deliver courses globally are emerging. Existing institutions are trying to change their teaching strategies in order to position themselves to deliver their courses more effectively on a global basis. Educators and technologists are predicting the further globalisation of education as more and more institutions, in the face of competition both real the perceived, adopt online technologies to teach globally.

Arguments that favour global distance education are mainly:

- the benefits to students of participating in a course with colleagues drawn from across the world,

- the provision of access to high quality education wherever a student lives
- the way that scarce, top quality expertise can be made available to students anywhere in the world,
- the provision of access to curricula that embrace a broader spectrum of knowledge than any one institution might accomplish,
- the search for new revenue in a global market place,
- the empowerment of learners who can choose courses from a range of institutions previously closed to them, and
- the cost-efficiency of course development—the development costs of a course can be shared across not just a local, national market, but across a global market.

Against the above arguments in favour of global distance education, certain concerns and dangers are expressed against it. A main concern is learner isolation as students learn from the screen and not through interaction with peers and teachers. Another concern is the reduction of education to a packaged consumer goods. Further concern is globalisation of content, with a consequential loss of cultural diversity and richness. Institutions that cross jurisdictional boundaries also face different legal and financial frameworks. Crossing national boundaries certainly add to the logistical and organisational problems of distance teaching institutions.

One of the problems facing global distance education providers is a concern that the new providers are more interested in profit than quality service. David Noble, a fierce critic of the commercialising tendencies of distance education, pointed out to the tendency of 19th and 20th century commercial distance education to rely on drop-out money for profit. He believes that commercial element in distance education is even stronger now.

Quality assurance frameworks for distance education in a globalised contexts are still in the early stages of development. Studies indicate the need for investigating a wide range of quality assurance practices in different contexts of distance education and discussing quality assurance matters in depth at the international level.

The UNESCO/OECD Guidelines on Quality Provision in Cross-Border Higher Education may provide a valuable reference for developing national guidelines.

In the context of the growing globalisation in distance education, there is an urgent need for international initiatives to review quality assurance mechanisms of distance education at the national and institutional level, to discuss new challenges facing a changing distance education environment, and to build quality assurance capacity to enhance quality standards in a globalized education market.

Perraton and Rumble, in the context of globalisation of distance education, raise a range of management problems, the major ones being:

- Designing an appropriate structure.
- Designing an appropriate technology strategy to underpin a global distance education programme.
- Devising procedures and frameworks that will provide a satisfactory and consistent level of service to students any time, any place.
- Devising an appropriate approach to enable distance education courses to be delivered globally across different cultures.
- Designing attractive service rules that will support the service delivery model, rather than working against it.
- Overcoming the logistical and organisational problems that arise when programmes are delivered transnationally.
- Managing intellectual property and copyright problems.
- Coping with the various and different legal frameworks that apply, including those affecting the transnational employment of staff.
- Coping with the problems posed by foreign exchange restrictions.
- Retaining a commitment to meet the needs of disadvantaged sectors of society – a commitment that may actually argue against some of the very technologies that make globalised distance education possible.

2. Mobile Learning (M-Learning)

M-learning or mobile learning is defined as "learning across multiple contexts, through social and content interactions, using personal electronic devices.". A form of e-learning distance education, M-learners can use mobile device educational technology in many locations at their time convenience.

M-learning technologies include handheld computers, MP3 players, notebooks, mobile phones and tablets. M-learning focuses on the mobility of the learner, interacting with portable technologies. Using mobile tools for creating learning aids and materials becomes an important part of informal learning.

M-learning is convenient in that it is accessible from virtually anywhere. Sharing is almost instantaneous among everyone using the same content, which leads to the reception of instant feedback and tips. M-learning also brings strong portability by replacing books and notes with small devices, filled with tailored learning contents.

Mobile learning is the delivery of learning, education or learning support on mobile phones, PDAs or tablets. E-Learning has provided the ability for traditional learning to break out of the classroom setting and for students to learn at home. Mobile learning has enhanced upon e-learning by taking it a step further and allowing students to learn virtually anywhere a mobile signal is available. This allows students to stay connected to the classroom while traveling, vacationing, during breaks or during any other free time one may have.

New mobile technology, such as hand-held based devices, is playing a large role in redefining how we receive information. The recent advances in mobile technology are changing the primary purpose of mobile devices from making or receiving calls to retrieving the latest information on any subject.

Mobile devices (such as a Pocket PC) in the classroom can be used to enhance group collaboration among students through communication applications, interactive displays, and video features.

Existing mobile technology can replace cumbersome resources such as textbooks, visual aids, and presentation technology.

Interactive and multi-mode technology allows students to engage and manipulate information.

Mobile Device features with WIFI capabilities allow for on-demand access to information. Access to classroom activities and information on mobile devices provides a continuum for learning inside and outside the classroom.

Mobile devices can be used in brick-and-mortar or online settings to enhance learning experiences.

The mobile phone (through text SMS notices) can be used especially for distance education or with students whose courses require them to be highly mobile and in particular to communicate information regarding availability of assignment results, venue changes and cancellations, etc. It can also be of value to business people, e.g. sales representatives who do not wish to waste time away from their busy schedules to attend formal training events. Mobile devices facilitate online interaction between instructor and student, and student to student.

Podcasting consists of listening to audio recordings of lectures. It can be used to review live lectures and to provide opportunities for students to rehearse oral presentations. Podcasts may also provide supplemental information to enhance traditional lectures.

Psychological research suggests that university students who download podcast lectures achieve substantially higher exam results than those who attend the lecture in person (in cases in which students take notes).

M-learning in a workplace can be very different from a school's context. Although employees do occasionally attend face to face training events, the majority of work-based learning happens on the job, often at the moment of need. Because of this, m-learning is being used in a wider range of modes:

- On the job training for someone who accesses training on a mobile device.
- Just in time training to solve a problem or gain an update.
- Performance support. Immediate access to tools to streamline a work-task
- Reference guides and ebooks
- Checklists

Due to the very diverse training needs across a large organisation, self-serve learning is more common than is found at the school, or college level. Mobile is seen as an effective way to reach a large number of employees easier and more effectively.

Value

The value of mobile learning—Tutors who have used m-learning programs and techniques have made the following value statements in favour of m-learning.

- It is important to bring new technology into the classroom.
- Devices used are more lightweight than books and PCs.
- Mobile learning can be used to diversify the types of learning activities students partake in (or a blended learning approach).
- Mobile learning supports the learning process rather than being integral to it.
- Mobile learning can be a useful add-on tool for students with special needs. However, for SMS and MMS this might be dependent on the students' specific disabilities or difficulties involved.

- Mobile learning can be used as a 'hook' to re-engage disaffected youth.

Benefits

- Relatively inexpensive opportunities, as the cost of mobile devices are significantly less than PCs and laptops
- Multimedia content delivery and creation options
- Continuous and situated learning support
- Decrease in training costs
- Potentially a more rewarding learning experience
- New opportunities for traditional educational institutions
- Readily available a/synchronous learning experience

Challenges

- Connectivity and battery life
- Screen size and key size
- Meeting required bandwidth for nonstop/fast streaming
- Number of file/asset formats supported by a specific device
- Content security or copyright issue from authoring group
- Multiple standards, multiple screen sizes, multiple operating systems
- Reworking existing E-Learning materials for mobile platforms
- Limited memory
- Risk of sudden obsolescence
- Security
- Work/Life Balance
- Cost of Investment
- Social and educational challenges include
  - Accessibility and cost barriers for end users: Digital divide.
  - How to assess learning outside the classroom
  - How to support learning across many contexts
  - Content's security or pirating issues
  - Frequent changes in device models/technologies/ functionality etc.
  - Developing an appropriate theory of learning for the mobile age
  - Conceptual differences between e-learning and m-learning
  - Design of technology to support a lifetime of learning
  - Tracking of results and proper use of this information
  - No restriction on learning timetable
  - Personal and private information and content

- ➢ No demographic boundary
- ➢ Disruption of students' personal and academic lives
- ➢ Access to and use of the technology in developing countries
- ➢ Risk of distraction

Over the past ten years mobile learning has grown from a minor research interest to a set of significant projects in schools, workplaces, museums, cities and rural areas around the world. The M-learning community is still fragmented, with different national perspectives, differences between academia and industry, and between the school, higher education and lifelong learning sectors. Possible future applications for Mobile Learning include location based learning, augmented reality, wearable learning, learning implants, and ambient intelligence. Advancements in Mobile Learning will require a change from traditional classroom pedagogical approaches to a digital pedagogical approach that will suit mobile learners.

3. Massive Open Online Courses (MOOCS)

A massive open online course is an online course aimed at unlimited participation and open access via the web. In addition to traditional course materials such as filmed lectures, readings, and problem sets, many MOOCs provide interactive user forums to support community interactions between students, professors, and teaching assistants (TAs). MOOCs are a recent and widely researched development in distance education which was first introduced in 2008 and emerged as a popular mode of learning in 2012.

Early MOOCs often emphasized open-access features, such as open licensing of content, structure and learning goals, to promote the reuse and remixing of resources. Some later MOOCs use closed licenses for their course materials while maintaining free access for students. The term MOOC was coined simultaneously by Dave Cormier and Bryan Alexander.

Early Approaches

The first MOOCs emerged from the open educational resources (OER) movement. The term MOOC was coined in 2008 by Dave Cormier of the University of Prince Edward Island in response to a course called Connectivism and Connective Knowledge (also known as CCK08). CCK08, which was led by George Siemens of Athabasca University and Stephen Downes of the National Research Council, consisted of 25 tuition-paying students in Extended Education at the University of Manitoba, as well as over 2200 online students from the general public who paid nothing.

All course content was available through RSS feeds and online students could participate through collabourative tools, including blog posts, threaded discussions in Moodle and Second Life meetings. Stephen Downes considers these so-called cMOOCs to be more "creative and dynamic" than the current xMOOCs, which he believes "resemble television shows or digital textbooks."

Emergence of MOOC Providers

According to *The New York Times*, 2012 became "the year of the MOOC" as several well-financed providers, associated with top universities, emerged, including Coursera, Udacity, and edX.

During a presentation at SXSWedu in early 2013, Instructure CEO Josh Coates suggested that MOOCs are in the midst of a hype cycle, with expectations undergoing wild swings. Dennis Yang, President of MOOC provider Udemy, later made the point in an article for the *Huffington Post*.

Many universities scrambled to join in the "next big thing", as did more established online education service providers such as Blackboard Inc, in what has been called a "stampede." Dozens of universities in Canada, Mexico, Europe and Asia have announced partnerships with the large American MOOC providers.

Instructional Design

Many MOOCs use video lectures, employing the old form of teaching (lecturing) using a new technology. Thrun testified before the President's Council of Advisors on Science and Technology (PCAST) that MOOC "courses are 'designed to be challenges,' not lectures, and the amount of data generated from these assessments can be evaluated 'massively using machine learning' at work behind the scenes. This approach, he said, dispels 'the medieval set of myths' guiding teacher efficacy and student outcomes, and replaces it with evidence-based, 'modern, data-driven' educational methodologies that may be the instruments responsible for a 'fundamental transformation of education' itself".

Industry

MOOCs are widely seen as a major part of a larger disruptive innovation taking place in higher education. In particular, the many services offered under traditional university business models are predicted to become unbundled and sold to students individually or in newly formed bundles.

These services include research, curriculum design, content generation (such as textbooks), teaching, assessment and certification (such as granting degrees) and student placement. MOOCs threaten existing business models by potentially selling teaching, assessment, and/or placement separately from the current package of services.

President Barack Obama has cited recent developments, including the online learning innovations at Carnegie Mellon University, Arizona State University and Georgia Institute of Technology, as having potential to reduce the rising costs of higher education.

Challenges and Criticisms

The MOOC Guide suggests 5 possible challenges for cMOOCs:

- Relying on user-generated content can create a chaotic learning environment
- Digital literacy is necessary to make use of the online materials
- The time and effort required from participants may exceed what students are willing to commit to a free online course
- Once the course is released, content will be reshaped and reinterpreted by the massive student body, making the course trajectory difficult for instructors to control
- Participants must self-regulate and set their own goals

Although the purpose of MOOCs is ultimately to educate more people, recent criticisms include accessibility and a Westernized curriculum that lead to a failure to reach the very audience they were intended to save.

Despite the criticisms, MOOCs like any disruptive technologies are evolving. They are gaining traction among motivated adult learners and in Third-World countries where the quality of education is questionable. Cost of present education is also creating debts for students and their families. The environment is fertile for MOOCs to grow and disrupt education.

4. Open Educational Resources (OER)

The history of OER goes back to 1994 when Wayne Hodgins first time used the term "learning objects" in the context of instructional design for developing digital materials. He emphasised the importance of designing and producing the digital materials in such a manner as to be reused easily in a variety of pedagogical situations. These efforts basically aimed at detailing metadata, context exchange and other strategies for the users to final and reuse the digital educational content (Wiley, 2007).

Subsequently to this, David Wiley in 1998 came with the concept of "Open Content" basically for professional development of experts in the educational community. This idea became more popular by the inter-net users. The idea of open "content" was based on basic principles of open/ free source of software acquisition movement and was widely applied to open content and the creation of widely adopting open license for content.

Larry Lessing and others in 2001 developed the idea of "Creative Common" and widely circulated a set of flexible licenses to improve the Open Publication License and thereby increasing the credibility and confidence to the open content community. Meanwhile, the Massachusetts Institute of Technology in 2001 also announced its "Open Course Ware" in initiative to publish nearly every course of the university for free public access and for non-commercial use. It not only pronounced to encourage taking up such projects at the instructional level but also outsourced such activities leading the MIT brand to the movement.

Subsequently in 2002 the term "Open Educational Resources" was first adopted at UNESCO's 2002 Forum on the Impact of Open Courseware for Higher Education in Developing countries funded by the Williams and Flora Hewlett Foundation. The Forum described the OER as below:

Definition of OER

A definition of OER from the William and Flora Hewlett Foundation is:

"OER are teaching, learning and research resources that reside in the public domain or have been released under an intellectual property license that permits their free use or re-purposing by others. OER include full courses, course materials modules, textbooks, streaming videos, tests, software and any other tools materials or techniques used to support access to knowledge".

OER refer to learning material such as:

- Learning objects (quizzes, cross word, puzzles, flash cards, animations, interactive maps, timelines, etc.).
- Audio lectures
- Audio Video lectures
- Images
- Sounds and music
- Entire course content collection of journal articles and institutional repositories
- Textbooks

Need for OER

The need for OER is mainly due to the following reasons:

- Access and Distribution of Learning Resources
- Capacity Building
- Collabourative Efforts
- Best Practices
- Research

OER Facilitate ODE

OER strengthen open and distance education in developing countries, where there is a real shortage of creating knowledge pool for developing useful courseware. They also empower such nations to build their capacity to participate effectors in producing the open courseware. OER facilitate the open and distance education system in the following ways:

- Repository of Learning Content
- E-Learning Initiatives
- Licensing under Creative Common
- Forum for Profession
- Consortium for Course Development
- Professional Growth

Rationale for OER

The William and Flora Hewlett Foundation acted as Champion of OER since 2001 when it began to support MIT Open Course Ware, arguing that:

> "At the heart of the movement towards OER is the simple and powerful idea that the world's knowledge is a public good and that technology in general and the Worldwide Web in particular provide an extraordinary opportunity for every one to share, use, and reuse it".

The Hewlett Foundation supported many OER initiatives worldwide, including that of UNESCO.

While the Hewlett Foundation articulated a high level rationale for OER, the OECD Centre for Educational Research and Innovation, in tis scoping and mapping study of OER, identified specific advantages for various stakeholders.

Governments can serve citizens through:

- Widening participation in higher education by expanding access to learning and reaching non-traditional learners.
- Promoting lifelong learning
- Bridging the gap between formal informal and non-formal learning

Institutions may benefit in a number of ways:

- Sharing knowledge in congruent with academic tradition
- Tax payer's money is leveraged through the free sharing of resources
- The cost of content development can be reduced and quality may be improved
- The public image of the institution may be enhanced and new students attracted
- With increasing competition, institutions need to identify new cost recovery models

Educators also stand to benefits:

- Sharing is an academic value
- Personal gains through increased reputation
- Gaining publicly or reaching the market more quickly may result in an economic advantage

Barriers to OER

The potential benefits are not without barriers

- Technical, such as lack of broadband access
- Economic, such as inadequate resources to invest in the necessary software and hardware
- Social, such as lack of skills needed to use technology
- Policy oriented, such as lack of academic recognition of the development of OER by teaching staff
- Legal, such as the time and expense associated with gaining permission to use third part owned copyrighted materials or its removal from material

ICDE Task Force on OER

The ICDE Task Force on OER (2008) developed a Report on OER which aimed at contributing to the global OER movement, adding specific ICDE flavour and value by adopting the sub and distance learning perspective rather than the mainstream content-in-classrooms perspective. The Report tackled subjects including:

- Availability/access
- Intellectual property rights
- Internationalisation versus localisation of content
- Support for learning communities
- Quality control
- Financing and sustainable business models
- Interfacing with conventional degree studies
- Opportunities for bridge-building between informal, non-formal and formal learning
- Diversity in target groups
- Misuse and benefits to institutions offering OER
- Potential for developing using OER
- Changing roles of public are private sectors

The aim of the Report is to serve as an aid to higher education and open distance learning institutions in their decision to introduce or not for introduce OER activities.

The ICDE Task Force report identified threats that OER could represent for open, flexible and distance learning institutions.

The ICDE Task Force Report is discussed, evaluated and advanced as one of the major themes in the ICDE 23rd World Conference held in June 2009 in Netherlands.

Trends in the Development of OER

The following trends in the development of OER are worth noting:

- Many OER projects at universities and colleges are beginning at the bottom being driven by students within a university.
- Most OER projects are using Creative Common Licence or UNO Freed Documentation License to license their content. Among Creative Common Users, the Attribution Non Commercial – Shave Alika option is the most popular.
- Projects like eGermany are making it leaser than ever to mission OER for use in settings where connections to the Internet are slow, expensive or unreliable.

- Projects like the open source edu Commons software are making it easier than ever to do Open CourseWare projects.
- Podcasting, screen casting and video casting are becoming increasingly popular as inexpensive ways to capture and distribute course content.
- Syndication formats like RSS and ATOM are becoming increasingly popular ways to distribute meta data and provide access to content.
- Folksonomic approaches to metadata and indexing OER are gaining in popularity with end users.

Annexure

Organizations, Associations and Journals of Distance Education

I. Organizations

S. No.	Name of the Organization	Website
1.	UNESCO	http://www.unesco.org
2.	European Distance Education Network (EDEN)	http://www.eden.bme.hu
3.	Athabasca University Centre for Distance Education	http://cde.athabascau.ca/
4.	Central Institute for Distance Education Research	http://www.fernuni-hagen.de
5.	German Institute for Distance Education	http://www.uni-tuebingen.de
6.	Instituto Universitario de Educacion a Distancia	http://www.iued.uned.es
7.	International Centre for Distance Learning (ICDL)	http://www.icdl.open.ac.uk
8.	Asian Association of Open Universities (AAOU)	http://www.aaou.net
9.	Commonwealth of Learning	http://www.col.org
10.	Consorcio-Red de Education A Distancia (CREAD)	http://www.cread.org
11.	The South African Institute for Distance Education (SAIDE)	http://www.saide.org.za
12.	International Council for Distance Education (ICDE)	http://www.icde.org
13.	The Global Distance EducationNet	http://www1.worldbank.org.disted.home.html
14.	The European Association of Distance Teaching Universities (EADTU)	http://www.eadtu.nl
15.	The Canadian Association for Distance Education (CADE)	http://www.cade.aced.ca
16.	The British Association for Open Learning (BAOL)	http://www.baol.co.uk

S. No.	Name of the Organization	Website
17.	The Global Development Learning Network (GDLN)	http://www.gdln.org
18.	The Open and Distance Learning Quality Council (ODLQC)	http://odlqc.org/oldqc.
19.	American Association for Collegiate Independent Study (AACIS)	http://www.aacis.org
20.	American Center for the Study of Distance Education (ACSDE)	http://www.ed.psu.edu/acsde/
21.	The American Distance Education Consortium (ADEC)	http://www.adec.edu/
22.	Consortium of Distance Education (CODE)	http://www.codenetwork.org
23.	Council for Higher Education Accreditation (CHEA)	http://www.chea.org
24.	Educause	http://www.educause.edu/
25.	Federal Government Distance Learning Association	http://fdgla.org/
26.	International Association for Continuing Education and Training (IACET)	http://www.facet.org
27.	The Distance Education and Training Council	http://www.detc.org
28.	University Continuing Education Association (UCEA)	http://www.ucea.edu/
29.	U.S. Distance Learning Association (USDLA)	http://www.org/
30.	Web-based Education Commission	http://www.hpcnet.org/ webcommission
31.	The Distance Learning Resource Network (DLRN)	http://www.dlrn.org/

II. Associations

1. African Council for Distance Education (ACDE)
2. Asian Association of Open Universities (AAOU)
3. Australasian Council on Open, Distance and E-learning (ACODE)
4. British Institute for Learning and Development
5. Canadian Network for Innovation in Education (CNIE)
6. Caribbean Association for Distance and Open Learning (CARADOL)

7. Colombian Association for Distance Higher Education (ACESAD)
8. Consortium International Francophone de Formation a Distance (CIFFAD)
9. Distance Education Association of New Zealand (DEANZ)
10. Distance Education Association of Southern Africa (DEASA)
11. Distance Education Association of Tanzania (DEATA)
12. European Association for Distance Learning (EADL)
13. European Association of Distance Teaching Universities (EADTU)
14. European Distance and E-Learning Network (EDEN)
15. European Federation for Open and Distance Learning (EFODL)
16. Ghanaian Distance Education Association (GHADEA)
17. Indian Distance Education Association (IDEA)
18. Inter-American Distance Education Consortium (CREAD)
19. International Council for Open and Distance Education (ICDE)
20. Jamaican Association for Distance and Open Learning (JADOL)
21. Malaysian Association of Distance Education (MADE)
22. National Association of Distance Education and Open Learning in South Africa (NADEOSA)
23. National Distance Education Council
24. Open and Distance Education Association of Malawi (ODEAMA)
25. Open and Distance Learning Association of Australia (ODLAA)
26. Pacific Islands Regional Association for Distance Education (PIRADE)
27. Papua New Guinea Association for Distance Education (PNGADE)
28. The West African Distance Education Association (WADEA)
29. Zambia Association for Distance Education (ZADE)
30. Zimbabwe National Association of Distance and Open Learning (ZINADOL)

III. Journals

S. No.	*Name of the Journal*	*Website*
1.	*The American Journal of Distance Education*	http://www.AJDE.com
2.	*Distance Education* (Australia)	http://www.tandf.co.uk/ journals/carfax/01587919.html
3.	*The Journal of Distance Education* (Canada)	http://www.cade-acde.ca/ en_pub.php
4.	*International Review of Research in Open and Distance Learning*	http://www.irrodl.org/
5.	*Open Learning* (UK)	http://www.tandff.co.uk/ journals/carfa

S. No.	Name of the Journal	Website
6.	*The Journal of Library Services for Distance Education*	http://www.westga.edu/~library/jlsde/
7.	*Online Journal of Distance Learning Administration*	http://www.westaga.edu/~distance/jmain11.html
8.	*Quarterly Review of Distance Education*	http://www.aect.org/Publications/default.htm
9.	*The USDLA Journal*	http://www.usdla.org/html.membership/publications.htm
10.	*Distance Educatior.com*	http://www.distance-education.com/etp/
11.	*The Chronicle of Higher Education*	http://chronicle.com/
12.	*EDUCAUSE Quarterly*	http://www.educause.edu/pub/eq/
13.	*International Journal of Instructional Media*	http://www.adprima.com/ijim.htm
14.	*TechKnowLogia*	http://www.TechKnowLogia.org/
15.	*European Journal of Open and Distance Learning*	http://www.eurodl.org
16.	*International Journal of E-Learning*	http://www.aace.org/pubs/ijel
17.	*Turkish Online Journal of Distance Education (TOJDE)*	http://tojde.anandolu.edu.tr/
18.	*British Journal of Educational Technology* (UK)	http://www.blackwellpublishing.com/journals/BJET/descript.htm
19.	*The Journal of Distance Learning* (New Zealand)	http://www.deanz.org.nz.htm#anchor1

References

Baath, A.J. (1979). *Correspondence Education in the Light of a Number of Contemporary Teaching Models.* Malma: Liber Hermods.

Baath, A.J. (1980). *Postal Two Way Communication in Correspondence Education.* Lund, Sweden: Glec up.

Baath, A.J. (1981). On the Nature of Distance Education. *Distance Education, 2(2).*

Bates, A.W. (2000). *Managing Technologies Change: Strategies for College and University Leaders.* San Fransico: Jossey Bass.

Bates, A.W. (2005). *Technology, E-Learning and Distance Education.* London: Routledge.

Beaudion, M.F. (2005). *Reflections on Research, Faculty and Leadership in Distance Educator.* Olunberg: Bibliothecks.

Beaudoin, M.F. (2003). Distance Education Leadership: for the New Century. *Online Journal of Distance Learning Administration* 6(2).

Berge, Z. and Mrozowski, S. (2001). Review of Research in Distance Education. *American Journal of Distance Education,* 15(3).

Bernard, R.M. (2004). A Methodological Morass; How we can improve Quantitative Research in Distance Education. *Distance Education,* 25(2).

Billings, D.M. (1988). A Conceptual Model of Correspondence Course Completion. *The American Journal of Distance Education* 12(2).

Childs, G.B. (1963). Supervised Correspondence Instruction. In *The Brandenburg Memorial Essays on Correspondence Instruction.* Madison: University of Wisconsin.

COL (1990). *Report on Round Table on Training Distance Education.* Vancouver: COL.

Coldeway, D.O. (1990). Methodological Issues in Distance Education. In M.G., Moore (ed) *Contemporary Issues in American Distance Education.* New York: Bergamot Press.

Cole, S., Coats M. and Lentell, H. (1986). Towards Good Teaching by Correspondence. *Open Learning* 1(1).

Cropley, A. and Kahl, T. (1983). Distance Education: A Psychological Analysis. *Distance Education* 4(1).

Cynthia, J. (1998) *Leadership in Continuing and Distance Education in Higher Education.* New York: Allyn & Bacon.

Cyrs T.E. (2001) *Evaluating Distance Learning Programmes and Courses.* (www.zianet.com/edaeyrs/evaluate-ds).

Daniel, J. and Mackintosh, W. (2003). Leading ODL Futures in the External Triangle: The Mega University Response to the Gredest Moral Challenge of our Age in MG. Moore and W.G. Andreson (eds). *Handbook of Distance Education.* London: Lawrence Erlbaum.

Daniel, J.S. (1996). *Mega universities and Knowledge Media.* London: Kogan Page.

Delling, R.M. (1985). *Towards a Theory of Distance Education.* Paper Presented at the ICDE World Conference, Melbourne: Australia.

Delling, R.M. (1975). Distant Study as an opportunity for learning. In Ljosa, E (ed). *The System of Distance Education.* Melmo: Hermods.

Dodds, T. and Youngman, F. (2004). Distance Education in Botswana: Progress and Prospects. *Journal of Distance Education,* 19(1).

Dohmen, G. (1967). *Das Fernstudium. Ein Neues Pedagogicsches Forschung Sund Arbeitsfeld.* Tubingen: Ziff.

Dunning, B.S.; Venkekerix, J.M. and Zabrowski, L.M. (1993). *Reaching Learners through Telecommunications: Management and Leadership Strategies for Higher Education.* San Fransisco: Jossey Bass.

Ehrmann, S.C. (2001). *Evaluation and Assessment: Articles and Related URLs.* Washington: TLT Group.

El Bushra, J. (1973). *Distance Teaching at University Level.* Cambridge: IEC

Fitzpatrick, J., Sanders, J. and Worthen, B. (2004). *Programmed Evaluation: Alternative Approaches and Practical Guidelines.* Upper Saddle River: Pearson.

Freeman, R. (1977). *Managing Open Systems.* London: Kogan Page

Gellman Danley, B and Fetzner M. (1998). Asking the Really Tough Questions: Policy, Issues for Distance Learning. *Online Journal of Distance Learning* 1 (1).

Gooler, D.D. (1979). Evaluating Distance Education Programms. *Canadian Journal of University Continuing Education 6 (1).*

Harry, K. (1989) (ed). *Higher Education Through Open and Distance Learning.* London: Routledge.

Holmberg, B. (1960). *On the Methods of Teaching by Correspondence.* Lund: Gleerup.

Holmberg, B. (1966). *On the Methods of Teaching by Correspondence.* Lund: Gleerup.

Holmberg, B. (1977). *Distance Education: A Survey and Bibliography.* London: Kogan Page.

Holmberg, B. (1985). *The Feasibility of a Theory of Teaching for Distance Education and a Proposed Theory.* Hegen: Fern Universitat.

Holmberg, B. (1986). A Discipline of Distance Education. *Journal of Distance Education* 1(1).

Holmberg, B. (1986). *Growth and Structure of Distance Education.* London: Croon Helm

Holmberg, B. (1989). *Mediated Communication as Component of Distance Education.* Hegan: Fern Universitat.

Holmberg, B. (1995). *Theory and Practice of Distance Education.* London: Routledge.

House, E. (1996). (ed). *New Directions in Educational Evaluation.* Lewes: Falmer Press.

Jegede O. and Okebukola, P. (2002). *The Re-Emergency of ODL in Nigeria and its Use for Transforming Education for National Development.* PCF 2002 at Durban.

Jegede, O.J. (1994). Distance Education Research Priorities for Australia: A Study of Opinions of Distance Educators and Practitioners. *Distance Education 15(2).*

Jung, I.S. (2004). Convergence and Diversity of Quality Assurance Systems in Distance Education. *The SNU Journal of Educational Research (13).*

Kaye, A and Rumble, G. (1978). *Distance Teaching for Higher and Adult Education.* London: Croom Helm.

Kaye, A. and Rumble, G. (1981) (eds). *Distance Teaching for Higher and Adult Education.* London: Croom Helm.

Keegan, D. (1986). *The Foundations of Distance Education.* London: Croom Helm.

Keegan, D. (1996). *Foundations of Distance Education.* London: Routledge Falmer.

Keegan, D. (1998). Theories of Distance Education: Introduction. In D. Sewart, D. Keegan and B. Holmberg (eds). *Distance Education: International Perspectives.* New York: Routledge.

Keegan, D. and G. Rumble (1982). The DTUs: An Appraisal. In G. Rumble and K. Harry (eds). *The Distance Teaching Universities.* London: Croon Helm.

Keegan, D. and Rumble, G (1982). The DTUs: An Appraisal. In G. Rumble and K. Harry (Eds). *The Distance Teaching Universities,* London: Croon Helm.

Kember, D. (1975). *Open Learning for Adults: A Model of Students Progress.* Englewood Cliffs: ET Publications.

Kemmis, S. (1980). Programme Evaluation in Distance Education: Against the technology viation Reason. *Open Campus,* (2).

King, J., Nugent, G. Eich, J., Mlinek, D. and Russel, E. (2000). A Policy Framework for Distance Education: A Case Study and Model. *DEOSNEWS* 10(10).

Knowles, M. (1978). *The Adult Learner.* Houston: Gulf Publishing.

Kobler, M and Bunker, E. (1997). Trends in Research and Practice. An Examination of the American Journal of Distance Education 1987-1995. *American Journal of Distance Education* 11(2).

Koul, B.N. and Kanwar, A. (2006). *Perspectives on Distance Education: Towards a Quality of Culture.* Vancouver: COL.

Kulaindaiswamy, V.C. (1995). Social Demand for Higher Education Asia: How Cost Effective is Open Universities. *Indian Journal of Open Learning.*

Latchem, C. and Hanna, D. (2001). *Leadership and Management in Open and Flexible Learning.* London: Kogan Page.

Lee, Y., Driscoll, M.P. and Nelson, D.W. (2004). The Past, Present and Future Research in Distance Education: Results of Content Analysis. *The American Journal of Distance Education* 18(4).

Lentel, H. (2004). Framing Policy for Open and Distance Learning. In H. Perraton and H. Lantell (eds). *Policy for Open and Distance Learning.* London: Rutledge and COL

Lewis, R. (1985). *How to Develop and Manage an Open Learning Scheme.* London: Charles worth & Co.

Lewis, R. (1986). What is Open Learning? *Open Learning 1(5).*

Lockwood, F. (1997). *Developing Staff-Instructional Material for Open and Flexible Learning.* Pre-ICDE Conference Workshop Report. Penn State University.

Mac Intosh, N.E. (1978). Evaluation and Institutional Research: The Problems Involved in Evaluating one Course or Educational Programme. *International Journal of Institutional Management in Higher Education* 2(1).

Mackenzie, O. and Christensen, E. (1971) (eds). *The Changing World of Correspondence Study: International Readings.* University Park: Penn State University.

Mackenzie, O.; Christensen, E and Rigby, P.H (1968). *Correspondence Instruction in the United States.* New York: McGraw Hill.

Marriot, S. (1981). *A Backstairs to a Degree: Demand for an Open University in Late Victorian England.* Leeds Studies in Adult and Continuing Education.

Martinez, R.; Liu, S.; Watson, W. and Bichel Meyeer, B. (2006). Evaluation of a Web-based master's Degree Programme: Lessons Learned from an Online Instructional Design and Technology Programme. *Quality Review of Distance Education* 7(3).

Mason, J. and Goodenough, S. (1981). Course Creation. In A. Kaye and G. Rumble (eds). *Distance Teaching for Higher and Adult Education.* London: Croom Helm

Mason, R. (1999). The Impact of Telecommunications. In K. Harry (ed) *Higher Education Through Open and Distance Learning.* World Review of Distance Education and Open Learning – Vol-I. London: Routledge.

Miller and Rice (1967). *Systems of Organization: The Control of Task and Sentient Boundaries.* London: Tavistock Publications.

Mishra, S. (1997). A Critical Analysis of Periodical Literature in Distance Education. *Indian Journal of Open Learning*, 6(1).

Mishra, S. (1998). Research: A Review of its Structure, Methodological Issues and Priority Areas. *Indian Journal of Open Learning* 7(3).

Moore, M.G. (1973). Towards a Theory of Independent Learning and Teaching. *Journal of Higher Education* (44).

Moore, M.G. and Keersley, G. (2005). *Distance Education: A Systems View.* Belmont, CA: Thomas Wadsworth.

Moore, M.G. (1977). *On a Theory of Independent Study.* Hegen: Fernuniversitat (ZIFF).

Naidu, S. (2004). *Researching Distance Education and E-Learning.* Papers present at the National Workshop as Research Methodology for Distance and Open Learning. New Delhi: IGNOU.

Neil, M.W. (1981) (ed). *Education of Adults at a Distance: A Report of the Open University Tenth Anniversary International Conference.* London: Kogan Page.

Northcott, P. (1978). Course Team: Some Theoretical Considerations with Particular Reference to Open University Experience. In P. Northcott *et al.* (eds). *Course Teams. South Asian Australian College External Studies Distance Education, Series No. 8.* Adelaide: College of Technical and Further Education.

Paul, R. (1990). Open Learning and Open Management. London: Kogan Page.

Perraton, H. (2000). *Open and Distance Learning in the Developing World.* London: Routledge.

Perry, W. (1976). *Open University: A Personal Account by the First Vice-Chancellor.* Milton Keynes: Open University Press.

Peters, O. (1971). *Texte Zum Hochscul Fernstiudium*. Weinheim: Beltz.

Peters, O. (1973). *Die Didaktische Strukur Des Ferunterrichts. Untersuchungen Zu EINER Industrialisierten Form Des Lehrens and Lernens*. Weinheim: Beltz.

Peters, O. (1998). Distance Teaching and Industrial Production: A Comparative Interpretations in Outline. In D. Sewart; D. Keegan and B. Holmberg (eds). *Distance Education: International Perspectives*. New York. Routledge.

Peters, O. (2001). *Learning and Teaching in Distance Education: Pedagogical Analysis and Interpretations in an International Perspective*. London: Kogan Page.

Peters, O. (2008). Transformation through Open Universities. In T. Evans., M. Haughey and D. Murphy (eds). *International Handbook of Distance Education*. London: Emerald.

Prasad, V.S. (1994). Staff Training for DE System: Some Issues. In K. Murali Manohar (ed). *Staff Training in Distance Education*. Warangal: Kakatiya University SDLCE.

Reardon, K.K. (1995). In Your Leadership Holding You Back? *Executive* 18 (6).

Reddi, U.V. and Mishra, S. (2005) (eds). *Perspectives on Distance Education: Educational Media in Asia*. Vancouver: COL.

Ram Reddy, G. (1987). Planning, Management and Monitoring of Distance Education. In *Distance Education,* Vol-I. Manila: Asian Development Bank.

Robert, D. (1996). Feedback on Assignments. *Distance Education* 17(1).

Robinson, B. (1998). A Strategic Perspective on Staff Development for Open and Distance Learning. In C. Latchem and F. Lockwoods (eds). *Staff Development in Open and Flexible Learning*. London: Routledge.

Rossi, P., Lipsey, M. and Freeman, H. (2003). *Evaluation: A Systemic Approach*. Newbury Park: Sage.

Rourke, L. and Szabo, M. (2002). A Content Analysis of the Journal of Distance Education (1986-2001). *Journal of Distance Education* 17(1).

Rowntree, D. (1992). Exploring Open and Distance Learning. London: Kogan Page.

Rumble, G. (1981). Evaluating Autonomous Multi Media Distance Learning System: A Practical Approach. *Distance Education,* 2(1).

Rumble, G. (1986). *The Planning and Management of Distance Education*. London: Croom Helm.

Rumble, G. and Harry, K. (1982). *The Distance Teaching Universities*. London: Croom Helm.

Rumble, G. and Harry, K. (1982). General Characteristics of the Distance Teaching Universities. In G. Rumble and K. Harry (eds). *The Distance Teaching University.* London: Croom Helm.

Saba, F. (2000). Evaluating Distance Education Programmes. *Distance Education Report* 4(4).

Saltberg, S. and Polyson, S. (1995). Distributed Learning on the www. *Syllabus* 9(1).

Scriven, B. (1991). Ten Years of Distance Education. *Distance Education* 12 (1).

Sewart, D. (1978). *Continuity of Concern for Students in a System of Learning at Distance.* Hagen: Fern University, (ZIFF)

Sewart, D. (1981). Distance Teaching: A Contradiction in Term. *Teaching at a Distance* (19).

Sewart, D., Keegan, D. and Holmberg (1983) (eds). *Distance Education: International Perspective.* London: Routledge.

Simpson, O. (2002). *Supporting Students in Online, Open and Distance Learning.* London: Kogan Page.

Simonson, M. (2004). In Case You are Asked: The Effectiveness of Education. *Quality Review of Distance Education,* 3(4).

Simonson, M. and Bauck, T. (2003). Distance Education in Policy Issues: Strategic Perspectives. In M.G. Moore and W.G. Anderson (eds). *Handbook of Distance Education.* Mahwah, NJ: Lawrence Erlbaum Associates.

Simonson, M., Smaldino, S., Albright, M. and Zvacek (2009). *Teaching and Learning at a Distance*. Boston: Pearson.

Sims, R.S. (1977). *An Enquiry into Correspondence Education Process: Policies, Principles and Practices in Correspondence Education Systems Worldwide.* UNESCO.

Smith, R. (1987). Growth and Scope of Distance Learning. In *Distance Education in Asia and Pacific*. Vol I. Manila: ADB.

Stone, J.C. (1995). Alternative Organisational Structure for Developing Multimedia Instructional Materials. *Educational Technology* 15(10).

Tait, A. (1987). *Papers for the Second International Workshop on Counselling in Distance Education.* Cambridge: Open University East Angelic.

Taylor, J.C. (2001). *Fifth Generation Distance Education. Higher Education Series Report No. 40.* Australia, Dept. of Higher Education.

Tuntstall, J. (1974) (ed). *The Open University Opens.* London: Routledge.

UNESCO (2002). *Open and Distance Learning: Trends, Policy and Strategy Considerations.*

Wedemeyer, C. (1987). Independent Study. In A. Knowles (Ed). *The International Encyclopedia of Higher Education.* Boston: Northeastern University.

Wedemeyer, C.A. (1971). Independent Study. In *The Encyclopedia of Education.* New York: The McMillan Co.

Woodley, A. and Kirkwood, A. (1986). *Evaluation in Distance Learning Paper* 10. *Resources in Education.* Eric Document No. ED 304122.

Woodley, A. and Parlett, M. (1983). Students Dropout. *Teaching at a Distance,* 24(3).

Zhang, W.Z., Tsui, C. and Jagede, G. (2000). *A Comparison of Distance Education in Selected Asian Open Universities.* (Proceedings of 14th Annual Conference of AAOU).

Index